Curly, Wavy, or Straight: The Coat Types of Doodle Dogs

Copyright Page

TITLE: Curly, Wavy, or Straight: The Coat Types of Doodle Dogs

1ST Edition

Table of Contents

Curly, Wavy, or Straight: The Coat Types of Doodle Dogs......................1

Chapter 1: Understanding Doodle Dogs 2

Chapter 2: Doodle Dogs for Allergy Sufferers 11

Chapter 3: Miniature Doodle Dogs 17

Chapter 4: Doodle Dogs for Families with Children 23

Chapter 5: Service and Therapy Doodle Dogs..................................... 29

Chapter 6: Sporting Doodle Dogs... 35

Chapter 7: Doodle Dogs for Seniors.. 41

Chapter 8: Doodle Dogs for Apartment Living 47

Chapter 9: Doodle Dogs with Unique Coat Colors............................. 53

Chapter 10: Doodle Dogs with Specific Coat Types............................ 59

Chapter 11: Doodle Dogs for Active Lifestyles 67

Curly, Wavy, or Straight: The Coat Types of Doodle Dogs

By Roberto Miguel Rodriguez and Bradley James Loch

Chapter 1: Understanding Doodle Dogs

Introduction to Doodle Dogs

Welcome to the world of Doodle dogs! If you're a dog owner looking for the perfect furry companion, then you've come to the right place. In this subchapter, we will introduce you to the fascinating world of Doodle dogs and explore various sub-niches within this breed.

Doodle dogs have gained immense popularity in recent years due to their unique characteristics and versatility. They are a crossbreed between a Poodle and another dog breed, resulting in a wide range of coat types, sizes, and temperaments. These charming dogs are known for their hypoallergenic qualities, making them an excellent choice for individuals with allergies.

For those looking for a smaller-sized Doodle, we will explore breeds like the Miniature Labradoodle or Mini Goldendoodle. These pint-sized pups are perfect for those living in apartments or condos and adapt well to smaller spaces.

If you have a family with children, you'll be pleased to know that there are Doodle breeds known for their friendly and gentle nature. These dogs make fantastic companions for kids and are known for their patience and love for playtime.

Some Doodle breeds excel in service and therapy work due to their intelligence, trainable nature, and calm temperament. These dogs can make a real difference in the lives of those in need, providing support and companionship.

For the active individuals out there, we will explore Doodle breeds that are perfect for an active lifestyle. These dogs have high energy levels and love outdoor activities like hiking or running. They are your ideal exercise partner!

If you're looking for a Doodle with a unique coat color, we've got you covered. From merle to phantom and parti-color variations, these rare and eye-catching coats will surely turn heads wherever you go.

We will also delve into the different coat types of Doodle dogs, catering to individuals with specific preferences. Whether you prefer curly, wavy, or straight coats, there is a Doodle breed out there for you.

Lastly, we will explore Doodle breeds suitable for older individuals and those living in smaller spaces like apartments. These dogs are low-maintenance, easy to train, and provide companionship without overwhelming their owners.

So, whether you're an allergy sufferer, a family with kids, an active individual, or someone with specific preferences, there is a Doodle dog out there for you. Get ready to embark on an exciting journey to find your perfect Doodle companion!

The History of Doodle Breeds

Doodle dogs have become incredibly popular in recent years, but do you know where they come from? The history of doodle breeds is an interesting one that traces back to the late 20th century when breeders began crossing Poodles with other breeds to create dogs with hypoallergenic coats and friendly temperaments.

The first known doodle breed is the Labradoodle, which was developed in the 1980s by Australian breeder Wally Conron. He crossed a Standard Poodle with a Labrador Retriever in an attempt to create a guide dog with a hypoallergenic coat for a blind woman whose husband had allergies. The result was a dog that not only had the desired coat but also possessed the intelligence and trainability of the Poodle and the friendly nature of the Labrador Retriever.

Following the success of the Labradoodle, breeders began experimenting with other Poodle crosses, leading to the creation of several other popular doodle breeds. The Goldendoodle, a cross between a Golden Retriever and a Poodle, quickly gained popularity for its friendly and gentle nature, making it an excellent companion for families with children.

As the demand for doodle breeds grew, breeders started exploring smaller-sized varieties to cater to different lifestyles and living arrangements. Miniature Labradoodles and Mini Goldendoodles emerged as popular choices for individuals living in apartments or condos due to their smaller size and adaptability to smaller spaces.

Doodle breeds also found their way into various niche categories. For individuals with allergies, hypoallergenic doodle breeds such as the Labradoodle and Goldendoodle became the perfect solution, as their curly or wavy coats produce less dander, reducing the risk of allergic reactions.

Many doodle breeds also excel in sports and activities, such as agility, flyball, and dock diving. Their athleticism and high energy levels make them ideal companions for active individuals who enjoy outdoor activities like hiking or running.

In addition to their physical attributes, doodle breeds are known for their unique coat colors and types. From rare merle and phantom variations to parti-color patterns, these dogs offer a wide range of options for those looking for something different and eye-catching.

Today, doodle breeds continue to gain popularity and are sought after for their hypoallergenic coats, friendly temperaments, and versatility. Whether you're looking for a family companion, a service or therapy dog, or a sporting partner, there's a doodle breed out there that will suit your specific needs and preferences.

Characteristics of Doodle Dogs

When it comes to choosing the perfect dog for your family, doodle breeds are a popular choice due to their charming personalities and unique coat types. In this subchapter, we will explore the characteristics of doodle dogs, catering to different niches and preferences of dog owners.

For individuals with allergies, hypoallergenic doodle breeds are a great option. These dogs have minimal shedding and produce less dander, making them suitable for allergy sufferers. Breeds such as the Labradoodle and Goldendoodle are known for their hypoallergenic coats, allowing families to enjoy the companionship of a dog without the worry of allergies.

For those looking for a smaller-sized doodle, miniature doodle breeds are an excellent choice. Miniature Labradoodles and Mini Goldendoodles are adorable and compact, making them ideal for individuals living in apartments or condos. Despite their smaller size, these doodles still possess the same friendly and gentle nature as their larger counterparts.

If you have children, doodle breeds known for their friendly and gentle nature are perfect companions. These breeds are patient, loving, and playful, making them great family pets. Whether it's the Labradoodle or the Goldendoodle, these doodles will form strong bonds with your children, providing them with endless joy and companionship.

For individuals seeking service or therapy dogs, certain doodle breeds are commonly trained for these roles. Their intelligence, trainable nature, and calm temperament make them perfect candidates for assisting individuals with disabilities or providing emotional support. These doodles excel in their roles, bringing comfort and aid to those in need.

If you're an active individual who enjoys outdoor activities, sporting doodle breeds are a great fit. These energetic and athletic dogs excel in various dog sports and activities such as agility, flyball, or dock diving. With their high energy levels, they will keep up with your active lifestyle and become your perfect adventure buddy.

Whether you're a senior or living in a smaller space like an apartment, there are doodle breeds suitable for your needs. Doodles that are smaller in size, have lower energy levels, and are easy to train are ideal for seniors. Similarly, certain doodle breeds adapt well to apartment living due to their size and exercise requirements, making them perfect for individuals with limited space.

Lastly, doodle breeds come in a variety of unique coat colors and types. From rare merle and phantom variations to parti-color combinations, these doodles stand out and make a fashion statement. Additionally, doodles with specific coat types such as curly, wavy, or straight cater to individuals with specific preferences, allowing them to find their perfect match.

In conclusion, doodle breeds possess a wide range of characteristics that cater to different niches and preferences of dog owners. Whether you're looking for a hypoallergenic companion, a smaller-sized doodle, a family-friendly pet, a service or therapy dog, an athletic partner, a suitable dog for seniors or apartment living, a unique coat color, or a specific coat type, there is a doodle breed out there for you. By understanding these characteristics, you can make an informed decision and find the perfect doodle dog to join your family.

Popular Doodle Breeds

Doodle dogs have gained immense popularity among dog owners due to their unique coat types and lovable personalities. In this subchapter, we will explore some of the most popular doodle breeds that cater to various niches and preferences within the dog owner community.

For individuals with allergies, hypoallergenic doodle breeds are a great choice. These breeds, such as the Labradoodle and Goldendoodle, have non-shedding coats that produce fewer allergens, making them suitable for allergy sufferers.

If you are looking for a smaller-sized doodle, Miniature Labradoodles and Mini Goldendoodles are perfect companions. These pint-sized bundles of joy still possess the same charming traits as their larger counterparts, but in a more compact package.

For families with children, doodle breeds known for their friendly and gentle nature are ideal. Breeds like the Bernedoodle and Australian Labradoodle are not only great with kids but also make excellent family pets due to their loyal and sociable personalities.

Doodle breeds like the Sheepadoodle and Goldendoodle are commonly trained as service or therapy dogs due to their intelligence, trainable nature, and calm temperament. These breeds excel in providing assistance and support to individuals in need.

If you are an active individual who enjoys outdoor activities, sporting doodle breeds are an excellent choice. Breeds like the Aussiedoodle and Labradoodle thrive in various dog sports and activities such as agility, flyball, and dock diving.

For seniors, doodle breeds that are suitable for older individuals are worth considering. Factors like size, energy level, and ease of training are taken into account when selecting breeds like the Cavapoo or Cockapoo that can provide companionship without being overwhelming.

If you live in a smaller space like an apartment or condo, there are doodle breeds that adapt well to such environments. Miniature Labradoodles and Cockapoos are known to be apartment-friendly due to their smaller size and exercise requirements.

For those who appreciate unique coat colors, there are doodle breeds with rare or unique coat variations. Breeds such as the Merle Labradoodle or Phantom Goldendoodle showcase stunning coat patterns that are sure to turn heads.

Lastly, doodle breeds with specific coat types cater to individuals with specific preferences. Whether you prefer a curly, wavy, or straight coat, there are doodle breeds like the Curly Labradoodle, Wavy Goldendoodle, or Straight Cockapoo that will meet your desires.

In conclusion, doodle breeds come in a variety of types and cater to various niches within the dog owner community. Whether you are looking for a hypoallergenic companion, a smaller-sized doodle, a family-friendly breed, or a sporting partner, there is a doodle breed out there that will capture your heart and fit your lifestyle perfectly.

Choosing the Right Doodle Dog for You

When it comes to finding the perfect furry companion, doodle dogs offer a wide variety of options to suit different lifestyles and preferences. Whether you are an allergy sufferer, a senior looking for a low-maintenance pet, or an active individual seeking a four-legged partner for outdoor adventures, there is a doodle breed out there that will fit your needs. In this subchapter, we will explore some of the different niches within the world of doodle dogs, helping you choose the right one for you.

For allergy sufferers, certain doodle breeds are known for being hypoallergenic and suitable for individuals with allergies. These breeds have non-shedding coats that produce less dander, making them a great choice for those with sensitivities.

If you are looking for a smaller-sized companion, miniature doodle dogs may be the perfect fit for you. Breeds such as Miniature Labradoodles or Mini Goldendoodles offer all the charm and personality of their larger counterparts in a more compact package.

Families with children will find certain doodle breeds to be excellent companions for their little ones. These breeds are known for their friendly and gentle nature, making them great playmates and family pets.

For those interested in service or therapy dogs, there are doodle breeds that are commonly trained for these roles. Their intelligence, trainable nature, and calm temperament make them well-suited for providing assistance and support to those in need.

If you are a sports enthusiast, sporting doodle breeds are the way to go. These dogs excel in various dog sports and activities, such as agility, flyball, or dock diving, and will keep up with your active lifestyle.

Seniors looking for a furry companion will find doodle breeds that are suitable for their needs. Factors such as size, energy level, and ease of training are taken into consideration to ensure a perfect match.

For those living in smaller spaces, such as apartments or condos, there are doodle breeds that adapt well to these environments. Their size and exercise requirements make them a great fit for apartment living.

Some doodle breeds come with unique coat colors, such as merle, phantom, or parti-color variations. These dogs are sure to turn heads wherever they go.

Lastly, if you lead an active lifestyle and enjoy outdoor activities like hiking or running, there are doodle breeds that will keep up with you. Their high energy levels and athleticism make them perfect companions for your adventures.

In conclusion, when choosing the right doodle dog for you, consider your specific needs, preferences, and lifestyle. With the wide range of doodle breeds available, you are sure to find the perfect match that will bring joy, companionship, and love to your life.

Chapter 2: Doodle Dogs for Allergy Sufferers

What Makes Doodle Breeds Hypoallergenic?

If you suffer from allergies but still dream of having a furry friend by your side, doodle breeds may be the perfect solution for you. These adorable dogs are known for their hypoallergenic qualities, making them suitable companions for individuals with allergies. But what exactly makes doodle breeds hypoallergenic?

The primary reason why doodle breeds are hypoallergenic is their coat type. Doodle dogs have a unique blend of genetics from their poodle and retriever ancestors, resulting in a variety of coat types such as curly, wavy, or straight. These coats are often low-shedding, which means they produce less dander – a common allergen found in pet hair and skin cells.

In addition to being low-shedding, doodle breeds also have a different type of hair compared to other dog breeds. Instead of having typical fur, doodles have hair that grows continuously, similar to human hair. This characteristic reduces the amount of loose hair and dander that may trigger allergies. However, it's important to note that no dog breed is completely hypoallergenic, as all dogs produce some level of allergens.

Another factor that contributes to the hypoallergenic nature of doodle breeds is their minimal oil production. Unlike other dog breeds, doodles have oil glands in their skin that are less active, resulting in less oil secretion. This is beneficial for allergy sufferers, as the oil can trap allergens in the dog's coat, potentially causing allergic reactions. With doodle breeds, the reduced oil production minimizes the accumulation of allergens on their skin and hair.

Regular grooming and maintenance are essential to keep doodle breeds hypoallergenic. Brushing their coat frequently helps remove loose hair and dander, preventing them from spreading around your home. Bathing your doodle regularly can also help reduce allergens on their skin and coat. Consulting with a professional groomer who is familiar with doodle breeds can provide you with valuable advice on the best grooming practices to maintain their hypoallergenic qualities.

In conclusion, doodle breeds are hypoallergenic due to their unique coat types, low-shedding nature, minimal oil production, and continuous hair growth. While no dog breed can guarantee a completely allergy-free environment, doodle breeds are often a great choice for individuals with allergies who still want to experience the joy and companionship of owning a dog.

Best Doodle Breeds for Individuals with Allergies

Subchapter: Best Doodle Breeds for Individuals with Allergies

If you're a dog owner with allergies, finding the right breed can be a challenge. However, doodle dogs are known to be hypoallergenic and suitable for individuals with allergies. In this subchapter, we will explore the best doodle breeds for allergy sufferers.

1. Labradoodle: Labradoodles are a cross between a Labrador Retriever and a Poodle. They are renowned for their hypoallergenic coat and are an excellent choice for individuals with allergies. Labradoodles come in various sizes, from standard to miniature, allowing you to find the perfect fit for your home.

2. Goldendoodle: Goldendoodles are a mix of Golden Retrievers and Poodles. These adorable dogs have a low-shedding coat, making them ideal for allergy sufferers. They are also known for their friendly and gentle nature, making them great companions for families with children.

3. Bernedoodle: Bernedoodles are a cross between Bernese Mountain Dogs and Poodles. With their hypoallergenic coat, they are a perfect choice for individuals with allergies. Bernedoodles are also known for their intelligence and trainability, making them suitable for service or therapy dog work.

4. Sheepadoodle: Sheepadoodles are a mix of Old English Sheepdogs and Poodles. These dogs have a curly or wavy hypoallergenic coat, making them a great option for individuals with allergies. Sheepadoodles are also known for their friendly and gentle nature, making them great companions for families with children.

5. Cavapoo: Cavapoos are a cross between Cavalier King Charles Spaniels and Poodles. These small-sized doodle breeds are perfect for individuals with allergies and limited space. Cavapoos are known for their affectionate and sociable nature, making them an excellent choice for families.

When considering a doodle breed for allergies, it's essential to remember that individual reactions may vary. It's always recommended to spend time with the breed before making a decision, as some individuals may still experience allergy symptoms despite the breed's hypoallergenic qualities.

In conclusion, if you're a dog owner with allergies, doodle breeds can be a fantastic option. Labradoodles, Goldendoodles, Bernedoodles, Sheepadoodles, and Cavapoos are just a few of the best doodle breeds for individuals with allergies. With their hypoallergenic coats and friendly nature, these dogs can bring joy and companionship to your life without triggering allergic reactions.

Grooming Tips for Allergy-Friendly Doodle Dogs

If you're a dog owner who suffers from allergies, owning a doodle dog can be a great option. Doodle breeds, such as Labradoodles or Goldendoodles, are known for being hypoallergenic and suitable for individuals with allergies. However, proper grooming is essential to keep these allergy-friendly dogs healthy and comfortable. In this subchapter, we will explore some grooming tips specifically tailored to allergy-friendly doodle dogs.

First and foremost, regular brushing is crucial for doodle dogs with curly, wavy, or straight coats. This helps to prevent matting and tangling, which can lead to skin irritation and discomfort. Use a slicker brush or a comb with wide teeth to remove any loose hair and keep the coat tangle-free. Aim to brush your doodle dog at least once a week, if not more often.

In addition to brushing, regular bathing is also important for allergy-friendly doodle dogs. Use a mild, hypoallergenic shampoo to avoid causing any skin irritations. Be sure to rinse thoroughly to remove all traces of shampoo from the coat. After bathing, gently towel dry your doodle dog and use a low heat setting on a blow dryer to finish the drying process. Avoid using high heat as it can damage the coat.

Trimming your doodle dog's hair is another essential grooming task. Regular haircuts help to keep the coat at a manageable length and prevent it from becoming too long and prone to matting. If you're not confident in trimming your dog's hair yourself, consider taking them to a professional groomer who specializes in doodle breeds.

Lastly, don't forget about the ears and nails of your allergy-friendly doodle dog. Clean the ears regularly using a gentle ear cleaner recommended by your veterinarian. Trim the nails regularly to prevent overgrowth and discomfort.

By following these grooming tips, you can ensure that your allergy-friendly doodle dog remains healthy, comfortable, and allergy-friendly. Remember, regular brushing, bathing, trimming, and ear and nail care are essential for maintaining your doodle dog's coat and overall well-being.

Living with a Doodle Dog as an Allergy Sufferer

If you're an allergy sufferer, owning a dog may seem impossible. However, there is good news for those who long for a furry companion but struggle with allergies – the hypoallergenic Doodle dog. Doodle breeds, such as Labradoodles and Goldendoodles, are known for their low-shedding and low-dander coats, making them a great option for individuals with allergies.

Living with a Doodle dog as an allergy sufferer can be a game-changer. These breeds have hair rather than fur, which reduces the amount of allergens they produce. Additionally, their curly or wavy coats trap dander, preventing it from floating around your home and triggering your allergies. However, it is important to note that while Doodle dogs are hypoallergenic, individual reactions may vary. It is always recommended to spend time with a Doodle dog before bringing one home to ensure you don't have any adverse reactions.

To create a comfortable living environment for both you and your Doodle dog, regular grooming is essential. Brushing your Doodle's coat frequently will help remove any loose hair and minimize dander. Bathing your Doodle regularly can also help reduce allergens on their skin and coat. It's important to use hypoallergenic shampoos and grooming products to further minimize the risk of triggering allergies.

In addition to their hypoallergenic qualities, Doodle dogs are also known for their friendly and gentle nature, making them suitable companions for families with children. Their intelligence and trainable nature also make them ideal candidates for service or therapy dog training. Doodle breeds excel in various dog sports and activities, making them perfect for active individuals who enjoy outdoor activities. However, it's important to consider their energy levels and exercise requirements when choosing a Doodle breed that suits your lifestyle.

Living in smaller spaces like apartments or condos is not a problem for Doodle dogs. Their adaptability and size make them ideal companions for apartment living. They require regular exercise, but a daily walk and some playtime indoors can keep them happy and healthy.

If you have specific preferences for coat colors or types, there are Doodle breeds that offer a range of options. From rare or unique coat colors like merle, phantom, or parti-color variations to specific coat types like curly, wavy, or straight, you can find a Doodle dog that suits your aesthetic preferences.

Living with a Doodle dog as an allergy sufferer is not only possible but can bring immense joy and companionship. These hypoallergenic and versatile breeds offer a range of options to cater to different lifestyles and preferences. With proper grooming and care, you can enjoy the company of a Doodle dog without worrying about allergies.

Chapter 3: Miniature Doodle Dogs

Introduction to Miniature Doodle Breeds

In this subchapter, we will explore the fascinating world of Miniature Doodle breeds. These smaller-sized doodle dogs have gained immense popularity among dog owners who are looking for a compact and adorable companion. Whether you live in a small apartment or simply prefer a smaller-sized dog, Miniature Doodles are the perfect fit.

Miniature Labradoodles and Mini Goldendoodles are two popular breeds within this sub-niche. These dogs are a cross between a Labrador Retriever or a Golden Retriever and a Miniature Poodle. The result is a charming and affectionate dog that possesses the best traits of both breeds.

What makes Miniature Doodles even more enticing is their hypoallergenic nature. For individuals who suffer from allergies, these breeds are a great choice as they have minimal shedding and produce less dander. This makes them suitable for households with allergy sufferers, allowing them to enjoy the companionship of a dog without the discomfort of allergies.

Miniature Doodles are also known for their friendly and gentle nature, making them excellent companions for families with children. They are patient and tolerant, making them great playmates for kids. Additionally, their intelligence and trainability make them suitable candidates for service and therapy work. Many Miniature Doodles excel in tasks such as emotional support, therapy, and assistance for individuals with special needs.

Despite their smaller size, Miniature Doodles are energetic and thrive in an active lifestyle. They enjoy outdoor activities like hiking, running, and agility sports. Their compact size also makes them well-suited for apartment living, as they adapt well to smaller spaces and have moderate exercise requirements.

Lastly, Miniature Doodles come in a variety of coat colors and types. From curly to wavy or straight, you can find a Miniature Doodle that matches your specific preferences. Some even have unique coat colors like merle, phantom, or parti-color variations, adding a touch of individuality to these already charming dogs.

In conclusion, Miniature Doodle breeds are a wonderful choice for dog owners who are looking for a smaller-sized, hypoallergenic, and friendly companion. Whether you have a family with children, an active lifestyle, or live in a smaller space, Miniature Doodles fit seamlessly into various lifestyles and bring immense joy and love to their owners.

Miniature Labradoodles: Characteristics and Care

Miniature Labradoodles are a popular choice among dog owners who are looking for a smaller-sized doodle breed. These adorable pups are a mix of a Labrador Retriever and a Miniature Poodle, resulting in a delightful combination of traits.

One of the most sought-after characteristics of Miniature Labradoodles is their hypoallergenic coat. This makes them a great choice for individuals with allergies, as they produce less dander and shed less hair compared to other breeds. Their curly or wavy coats require regular grooming to prevent matting, but their low shedding nature makes them easier to maintain for allergy sufferers.

Not only are Miniature Labradoodles hypoallergenic, but they are also known for their friendly and gentle nature. They are fantastic companions for families with children, as they are patient and love to play. However, it is important to supervise interactions between young children and dogs to ensure mutual respect and safety.

Miniature Labradoodles are intelligent and trainable, which makes them suitable candidates for service and therapy work. Their temperament and ability to learn quickly make them ideal for assisting individuals with disabilities or providing emotional support. Their small size also allows them to easily navigate various environments, making them versatile working dogs.

While Miniature Labradoodles are small in size, they have high energy levels and require regular exercise. They enjoy daily walks, play sessions, and mental stimulation to keep them happy and healthy. However, their exercise requirements can be adapted to apartment living, making them suitable for individuals living in smaller spaces.

When it comes to their coat types, Miniature Labradoodles can have either curly, wavy, or straight hair. This offers a range of options for individuals with specific preferences. Curly coats require more frequent grooming to prevent matting, while straight coats may require less maintenance.

In conclusion, Miniature Labradoodles are a wonderful choice for dog owners who are looking for a smaller-sized doodle breed. Their hypoallergenic coat, friendly nature, trainability, and adaptability make them suitable for various niches, including allergy sufferers, families with children, service and therapy work, apartment living, and individuals with specific coat preferences. However, it is important to remember that every dog is unique, and proper care, training, and socialization are essential for a happy and well-rounded Miniature Labradoodle.

Mini Goldendoodles: Traits and Training

Mini Goldendoodles are a popular choice for dog owners looking for a smaller-sized doodle breed that combines the best traits of the Golden Retriever and the Poodle. These adorable dogs have become increasingly sought after due to their hypoallergenic coats and friendly, gentle nature, making them suitable for a variety of niches, including families with children, seniors, and individuals with allergies.

One of the key traits of Mini Goldendoodles is their hypoallergenic coats, which make them an excellent choice for individuals with allergies. Their coats, which can be curly, wavy, or straight, are less likely to trigger allergies as they shed less dander and are less likely to cause allergic reactions. This makes Mini Goldendoodles a perfect fit for the niche of doodle dogs for allergy sufferers, allowing individuals with allergies to enjoy the companionship of a dog without worrying about their allergies.

In addition to their hypoallergenic coats, Mini Goldendoodles are known for their friendly and gentle nature, which makes them great companions for families with children. These dogs are typically very patient and tolerant, making them ideal playmates for kids. They are also highly trainable and intelligent, making them suitable for service and therapy work. Their temperament and intelligence make them a perfect fit for the niche of doodle dogs for families with children and service and therapy doodle dogs.

When it comes to training, Mini Goldendoodles are generally easy to train due to their intelligence and desire to please their owners. They respond well to positive reinforcement techniques and enjoy learning new tricks and commands. However, it's important to start training early and be consistent to ensure that they develop good manners and become well-behaved companions.

In conclusion, Mini Goldendoodles are a versatile breed that offers a range of traits and benefits for dog owners. Their hypoallergenic coats, friendly nature, and trainability make them suitable for individuals with allergies, families with children, and those looking for service or therapy dogs. Their smaller size also makes them a great fit for apartment living or for individuals with active lifestyles. If you're looking for a doodle breed that combines the best of the Golden Retriever and the Poodle in a smaller package, the Mini Goldendoodle may be the perfect choice for you.

Miniature Doodle Dogs as Family Pets

When it comes to finding the perfect family pet, many dog owners turn to miniature doodle dogs. These smaller-sized doodle breeds, such as Miniature Labradoodles or Mini Goldendoodles, are known for their friendly and gentle nature, making them great companions for families with children.

One of the main advantages of miniature doodle dogs as family pets is their size. They are smaller than standard doodle breeds, which means they take up less space in the home and are easier to handle, especially for younger children. Their compact size also makes them ideal for families living in apartments or condos, as they adapt well to smaller living spaces.

In addition to their size, miniature doodle dogs are also known for their intelligence and trainability. This makes them excellent candidates for families looking to include their furry friend in various activities and training sessions. Whether it's obedience training, agility, or even therapy work, these doodle breeds are quick to learn and eager to please.

Another advantage of miniature doodle dogs as family pets is their hypoallergenic coat. Many doodle breeds have a curly or wavy coat, which tends to shed less and produce less dander, making them suitable for individuals with allergies. This means that even allergy sufferers can enjoy the love and companionship of a family pet without the worry of triggering their allergies.

Furthermore, miniature doodle dogs are known for their affectionate and gentle nature towards children. They are patient and tolerant, making them great playmates for kids of all ages. Additionally, their high energy levels and athleticism make them suitable for active families who enjoy outdoor activities like hiking or running.

In conclusion, miniature doodle dogs make excellent family pets due to their small size, friendly nature, trainability, hypoallergenic coat, and compatibility with active lifestyles. Whether you have children, live in an apartment, or have allergies, these doodle breeds are a perfect fit for any family looking for a loving and loyal companion.

Chapter 4: Doodle Dogs for Families with Children

Doodle Breeds Known for Their Family-Friendly Nature

When it comes to finding the perfect family dog, doodle breeds are a popular choice due to their friendly and gentle nature. These lovable dogs are known for their affectionate personalities, making them great companions for families with children. In this subchapter, we will explore doodle breeds that are renowned for their family-friendly nature and discuss why they make excellent pets for households with kids.

One doodle breed that stands out in terms of its family-friendly nature is the Labradoodle. This crossbreed between a Labrador Retriever and a Poodle is not only highly intelligent but also incredibly friendly and patient, which makes them ideal for families with children of all ages. Labradoodles are known for their playful and gentle nature, and they thrive in an environment where they can be actively involved in family activities.

Another doodle breed that is perfect for families is the Goldendoodle. These adorable dogs are a mix between a Golden Retriever and a Poodle, combining the friendly and loyal nature of the Golden Retriever with the intelligence and low-shedding coat of the Poodle. Goldendoodles are known for their affectionate and patient temperament, which makes them great companions for children. They are also highly adaptable and can easily adjust to different living environments, making them suitable for families living in apartments or houses with a yard.

The Bernedoodle is another doodle breed that is well-suited for families with children. This crossbreed between a Bernese Mountain Dog and a Poodle is not only adorable but also known for its gentle and loving nature. Bernedoodles are highly sociable dogs that get along well with children and other pets. They are also intelligent and easily trainable, which makes them perfect for families looking for a dog that can participate in various activities and sports.

In conclusion, doodle breeds are an excellent choice for families looking for a friendly and gentle dog. Labradoodles, Goldendoodles, and Bernedoodles are just a few examples of doodle breeds known for their family-friendly nature. These dogs not only bond well with children but also bring joy and love to their families. So, if you are searching for a furry companion for your family, consider a doodle breed that will bring happiness and endless cuddles into your home.

Training and Socializing Doodle Dogs with Children

When it comes to choosing a family dog, doodle breeds are a popular choice due to their friendly and gentle nature. Doodle dogs, such as Labradoodles or Goldendoodles, are known for their intelligence and trainable nature, making them great companions for families with children.

When bringing a doodle dog into a household with children, it is important to focus on training and socializing them properly. This subchapter will provide valuable insights and tips on how to train and socialize doodle dogs with children.

First and foremost, it is crucial to establish a consistent and positive training routine. Doodle dogs are highly intelligent and eager to please, making them quick learners. Positive reinforcement techniques, such as rewards and praise, work best when training doodles. Teaching basic commands like sit, stay, and come will not only ensure the safety of the children but also create a well-behaved and obedient pet.

Socializing doodle dogs with children is equally important. It is essential to introduce the dog to children of different ages and sizes in a controlled environment. This will help the doodle become comfortable and accustomed to the presence of children and their unpredictable behaviors. Encouraging gentle interactions and rewarding calm behavior will reinforce positive associations with children.

Supervision is key when doodle dogs and children are interacting. While doodles are generally known for their gentle nature, accidents can still happen, especially with young children who may unintentionally provoke or mishandle the dog. Teaching children how to approach and interact with the dog safely, such as avoiding rough play or pulling on the dog's ears, is crucial for a harmonious relationship.

Additionally, incorporating regular exercise and playtime into the routine will help fulfill the doodle dog's energy needs, making them calmer and more relaxed around children. Activities such as interactive games, walks, and even involving the children in training sessions can strengthen the bond between the doodle and the family.

In summary, training and socializing doodle dogs with children requires patience, consistency, and positive reinforcement. By following these guidelines, dog owners can ensure a harmonious and safe environment for both the doodle and the children. Doodle breeds, with their friendly and gentle nature, can be excellent companions for families with children, bringing joy and love to the entire household.

Tips for Introducing a Doodle Dog to Your Family

Bringing a new dog into your family is an exciting time, and when that dog happens to be a lovable doodle breed, it's even more special. Doodle dogs, known for their friendly and gentle nature, make great companions for families with children. However, introducing a new furry friend to your family requires careful planning and preparation. Here are some tips to ensure a smooth transition for both your family and your new doodle dog.

1. Research the breed: Before bringing a doodle dog into your family, it's important to research the specific breed you're interested in. Each doodle breed has its own unique traits and characteristics, so understanding their needs and temperament will help you make an informed decision.

2. Create a safe space: Set up a designated area in your home where your doodle dog can feel safe and secure. This could be a crate, a cozy corner, or a specific room. Make sure the space is comfortable and equipped with essential supplies, such as food and water bowls, toys, and a comfortable bed.

3. Introduce gradually: When introducing your doodle dog to your family, take it slowly. Start by allowing your dog to explore one room at a time, gradually introducing them to other family members. This will help your dog feel less overwhelmed and give them time to adjust to their new surroundings.

4. Set boundaries: Establish clear boundaries and rules for your doodle dog from the beginning. This will help them understand what is expected of them and prevent any confusion. Consistency is key when it comes to training, so make sure everyone in the family is on the same page.

5. Socialize your doodle dog: Doodle dogs are known for their sociable nature, but it's important to expose them to different environments, people, and other animals early on. This will help them develop good social skills and become well-adjusted members of your family.

6. Provide mental and physical stimulation: Doodle dogs are intelligent and energetic, so it's essential to provide them with mental and physical stimulation. Regular exercise, interactive toys, and training sessions will keep them happy and prevent boredom.

7. Seek professional help if needed: If you're struggling with the introduction process or any behavioral issues, don't hesitate to seek professional help. A dog trainer or behaviorist can provide guidance and

support to ensure a successful integration of your doodle dog into your family.

By following these tips, you can create a loving and harmonious environment for your doodle dog and your family. Enjoy the journey of welcoming a new four-legged member into your home and cherish the moments you'll share together.

Activities and Playtime with Doodle Dogs and Kids

When it comes to finding the perfect family pet, doodle dogs are an excellent choice. Known for their friendly and gentle nature, doodle breeds make great companions for families with children. In this subchapter, we will explore the various activities and playtime ideas that can help strengthen the bond between doodle dogs and kids.

Doodle breeds, such as Labradoodles and Goldendoodles, are not only hypoallergenic but also highly adaptable to different environments. This makes them ideal for families with allergy sufferers or those living in smaller spaces like apartments or condos. Despite their size, doodle dogs have a remarkable ability to adjust their energy levels to match those of their owners, including kids.

One activity that doodle dogs and kids can enjoy together is going for long walks or hikes. Doodle breeds are known for their athleticism and high energy levels, making them perfect companions for active individuals and families. Whether it's exploring local parks or hiking trails, doodle dogs will eagerly join in on the adventure.

Another fun activity for doodle dogs and kids is playing fetch. Doodle breeds are highly intelligent and trainable, so teaching them to retrieve a ball or a frisbee can be a rewarding experience for both the dog and the child. This game not only provides physical exercise but also strengthens the bond between the two.

Doodle dogs also excel in various dog sports and activities. If your child is interested in agility, flyball, or dock diving, a doodle breed might be the perfect partner. These sports require agility, speed, and intelligence – all traits that doodle dogs possess.

It's important to remember that doodle dogs, like any other breed, require proper socialization and training. Involving kids in the training process can be a great learning experience for both the child and the dog. Teaching basic commands, such as sit, stay, and come, can help establish a strong bond and create a well-behaved and obedient pet.

In conclusion, doodle dogs are an ideal choice for families with children. Their friendly and gentle nature, combined with their intelligence and adaptability, make them excellent companions for kids. Engaging in activities and playtime with doodle dogs not only provides physical exercise but also strengthens the bond between the dog and the child. Whether it's going for long walks, playing fetch, or participating in dog sports, doodle dogs and kids can create lasting memories together.

Chapter 5: Service and Therapy Doodle Dogs

Doodle Breeds Suitable for Service Dog Work

When it comes to service dog work, it is crucial to find a breed that possesses not only the right temperament but also the intelligence and trainability required for such demanding tasks. Doodle breeds, with their unique mix of Poodle and other breeds, are often well-suited for this type of work.

One doodle breed that stands out for service dog work is the Labradoodle. Known for their intelligence and friendly nature, Labradoodles are commonly trained as service dogs to assist individuals with disabilities. Their hypoallergenic coats make them suitable for allergy sufferers as well. These dogs excel in tasks such as mobility assistance, guide work, and even therapy work due to their gentle and patient demeanor.

Another breed worth considering for service dog work is the Goldendoodle. These playful and intelligent dogs are often used as therapy dogs due to their calm and affectionate nature. Goldendoodles are also hypoallergenic, making them a great choice for individuals with allergies. With their versatility and eagerness to please, Goldendoodles can be trained for a wide range of tasks, including emotional support and medical alert work.

For those looking for a smaller-sized service dog, the Mini Labradoodle or Mini Goldendoodle might be the perfect fit. These pint-sized versions of their standard counterparts still possess the same intelligence and trainable nature, making them suitable for tasks such as hearing alert or medical response work. Their compact size also allows them to accompany their owners in various settings, including public transportation and crowded areas.

Another doodle breed that deserves recognition for service dog work is the Bernedoodle. These gentle giants have a calm and patient temperament, making them ideal candidates for therapy or emotional support work. With their hypoallergenic coat and striking tri-color markings, Bernedoodles are not only functional but also visually appealing.

When it comes to service and therapy doodle dogs, it is essential to remember that each individual dog's temperament and training potential should be assessed on a case-by-case basis. However, doodle breeds in general offer a combination of intelligence, trainability, and temperament that make them well-suited for service dog work. Whether you are in need of a mobility assistance dog, a therapy dog, or any other type of service dog, considering a doodle breed could be a wise choice.

Training and Temperament Required for Service Doodle Dogs

When it comes to service and therapy dogs, doodle breeds are often at the top of the list. Their intelligence, trainable nature, and gentle temperament make them ideal candidates for these important roles. If you're considering a service doodle dog, it's essential to understand the training and temperament requirements involved.

First and foremost, service doodle dogs need to undergo extensive training to perform their duties effectively. This training typically starts at a young age and covers basic obedience commands, specialized tasks, and socialization. Since doodles are known for their intelligence, they usually pick up commands quickly and thrive in training environments.

Additionally, service doodle dogs must possess a calm and gentle temperament. They need to remain composed in various situations and be able to handle stress with ease. This temperament is essential to ensure they can assist individuals with disabilities or provide comfort as therapy dogs. Doodle breeds, such as Labradoodles or Goldendoodles, are often selected for these roles due to their friendly and people-oriented nature.

Furthermore, service doodle dogs should have a strong bond with their handlers. This bond is built through consistent training, positive reinforcement, and regular interaction. It is crucial for the handler to establish themselves as a trusted leader, as this will enhance the dog's ability to perform tasks and provide support.

In terms of physical requirements, service doodle dogs should be in good health and have a suitable energy level for their specific duties. Some service tasks may require a higher energy level, while others may demand more focus and calmness. It is important to consider the individual's needs and match them with a doodle breed that aligns with those requirements.

Ultimately, service doodle dogs play an invaluable role in society, providing assistance and emotional support to those in need. Their training and temperament make them well-suited for these roles, and their intelligence and gentle nature make them wonderful companions. If you're considering a service doodle dog, ensure you are prepared to invest time and effort into their training and provide them with the love and care they deserve.

How Doodle Dogs Make Excellent Therapy Companions

Doodle dogs have gained immense popularity in recent years, and for good reason. These adorable crossbreeds, a mix of Poodles and other breeds like Labradors or Golden Retrievers, possess a unique combination of traits that make them exceptional therapy companions.

In this subchapter, we will explore why doodle dogs are perfect for individuals seeking therapy dogs, whether it be for emotional support or specific therapeutic purposes.

One of the key reasons why doodle dogs excel as therapy companions is their hypoallergenic coat. For individuals with allergies, finding a dog that doesn't trigger their symptoms can be a challenging task. However, many doodle breeds, such as the Labradoodle or Goldendoodle, have coats that are low-shedding and produce minimal dander. This makes them suitable for allergy sufferers who still desire the companionship and comfort that a therapy dog can provide.

Furthermore, doodle dogs are known for their friendly and gentle nature, making them great companions for families with children. Their patient and tolerant demeanor allows them to interact well with kids, providing a source of comfort and support. Doodle breeds like the Miniature Labradoodle or Mini Goldendoodle are particularly well-suited for families with limited space, as their smaller size allows them to adapt well to apartment living.

In addition to their friendly nature, doodle dogs possess high intelligence and trainability, making them ideal candidates for service or therapy dog training. Their willingness to learn and please their owners allows them to excel in various therapeutic roles, such as assisting individuals with physical disabilities, providing emotional support to those with mental health conditions, or even participating in animal-assisted therapy programs.

Moreover, doodle breeds are versatile and adaptable, excelling in a wide range of dog sports and activities. Whether it be agility, flyball, or dock diving, doodle dogs have the energy levels and athleticism required to participate and thrive in these activities. This makes them excellent choices for individuals with active lifestyles who enjoy outdoor activities and are looking for a furry companion to join them on their adventures.

In conclusion, doodle dogs possess a unique combination of traits that make them excellent therapy companions. Their hypoallergenic coats, friendly and gentle nature, high intelligence, and trainability, as well as their versatility in various dog sports and activities, make them perfect for individuals seeking therapy dogs. Whether you're an allergy sufferer, a family with children, or someone in need of emotional support, a doodle dog can provide the companionship and therapeutic benefits you're looking for.

The Benefits of Having a Service or Therapy Doodle Dog

For individuals in need of service or therapy dogs, doodle breeds have proven to be an excellent choice. These intelligent and trainable dogs possess the perfect combination of temperament and abilities to assist and support those who require additional aid. Whether it is for emotional support, physical assistance, or therapy purposes, service and therapy doodle dogs offer numerous benefits to their owners and the wider community.

One of the key advantages of having a service or therapy doodle dog is their intelligence. Doodle breeds, such as Labradoodles and Goldendoodles, are known for their high level of intelligence, making them quick learners. This intelligence allows them to be easily trained for specific tasks and commands necessary for their role as a service or therapy dog. From retrieving medication to providing comfort during stressful situations, these dogs can adapt to various needs and provide invaluable assistance.

Additionally, doodle breeds have a naturally friendly and gentle nature, which is essential for service and therapy work. Their temperament enables them to remain calm and composed in challenging situations, providing a sense of reassurance and comfort to their owners. This gentle nature also makes them well-suited for families with children, as they are patient and tolerant, making them ideal companions for young ones.

Service and therapy doodle dogs also possess a hypoallergenic coat, making them suitable for individuals with allergies. This unique characteristic reduces the risk of triggering allergic reactions, allowing those with allergies to benefit from the companionship and assistance of a service or therapy dog without compromising their health.

Moreover, these dogs excel in providing emotional support and companionship. Their presence can help alleviate anxiety, depression, and loneliness, making them valuable partners for individuals struggling with mental health issues. This emotional support can significantly improve the overall well-being and quality of life for their owners.

In conclusion, service and therapy doodle dogs offer a multitude of benefits to their owners. Their intelligence, gentle nature, hypoallergenic coat, and emotional support capabilities make them ideal companions for those in need. Whether it is assisting with daily tasks or providing emotional comfort, these dogs have proven to be invaluable assets in various therapeutic settings. If you are considering a service or therapy dog, exploring the world of doodle breeds is a worthwhile endeavor.

Chapter 6: Sporting Doodle Dogs

Athleticism and Agility in Doodle Breeds

When it comes to finding the perfect dog companion, many individuals seek out breeds that possess athleticism and agility. Doodle breeds, with their unique combination of Poodle and other breeds, can offer just that. In this subchapter, we will explore the doodle breeds that excel in these areas, making them ideal for active individuals who enjoy outdoor activities such as hiking or running.

One of the standout characteristics of doodle breeds is their high energy levels. Whether it's a Goldendoodle, Labradoodle, or any other doodle variation, these dogs are known for their boundless enthusiasm and zest for life. This energy translates into their athleticism, as they have the drive to participate in various dog sports and activities.

Agility is another area where doodle breeds shine. With their intelligence and trainable nature, they are quick learners and excel in agility training. Their athleticism allows them to navigate obstacles with ease, showcasing their agility and grace. Whether it's navigating a agility course, competing in flyball, or diving into water for dock diving competitions, doodle breeds are up for the challenge.

For dog owners with an active lifestyle, doodle breeds can be the perfect companion. Their high energy levels and athleticism make them great partners for outdoor activities. Whether it's going for a jog, hiking through rugged terrains, or playing a game of fetch in the park, doodle breeds will keep up with their owners every step of the way.

Furthermore, the intelligence and trainability of doodle breeds make them suitable for various training programs. They can be easily trained for off-leash walks, agility courses, or even as search and rescue dogs.

Their willingness to learn and please their owners make them a popular choice for individuals seeking a dog with both athleticism and intelligence.

In conclusion, doodle breeds are a fantastic choice for individuals with an active lifestyle. Their high energy levels, athleticism, and trainability make them ideal companions for outdoor activities and various dog sports. Whether it's hiking, running, or participating in agility competitions, doodle breeds will be by your side, ready to tackle any challenge.

Doodle Dogs in Competitive Dog Sports

For dog owners who are looking for a furry companion that can excel in various dog sports and activities, doodle breeds are an excellent choice. These intelligent and trainable dogs have the perfect combination of athleticism and eagerness to please, making them competitive contenders in the world of dog sports.

Doodle breeds such as Labradoodles and Goldendoodles have become increasingly popular among dog owners who enjoy participating in activities like agility, flyball, or dock diving. These sports not only provide mental and physical stimulation for dogs but also strengthen the bond between the owner and their furry friend.

Agility is a sport that involves navigating an obstacle course, testing a dog's speed, agility, and obedience. Doodle breeds, with their natural athleticism and intelligence, are quick learners and can easily master the agility course with the proper training and guidance.

Flyball is another exciting sport that doodle dogs can excel in. It is a relay race where dogs must jump over hurdles, retrieve a ball, and then race back to the start line. Doodle breeds, known for their high energy levels, love the thrill of the race and can quickly become star players in the flyball team.

Dock diving is a water sport where dogs jump off a dock into a pool of water, showcasing their strength and jumping ability. Doodle breeds, with their love for water and their natural athleticism, often make a big splash in this sport, impressing judges and spectators alike.

When it comes to competitive dog sports, doodle breeds have what it takes to shine. Their intelligence, trainability, and athleticism make them excellent competitors in activities like agility, flyball, and dock diving. Not only do these sports provide an outlet for their energy, but they also strengthen the bond between dog and owner.

If you are a dog owner looking to get involved in competitive dog sports, consider a doodle breed as your companion. They will not only bring joy and excitement to your life but also make you proud as they showcase their skills and talents in the sporting arena. So, grab your training gear and get ready to embark on an extraordinary journey with your doodle dog in the world of competitive dog sports.

Training Techniques for Sporting Doodle Dogs

In this subchapter, we will explore the various training techniques that are effective for sporting doodle dogs. These doodle breeds excel in various dog sports and activities, such as agility, flyball, or dock diving. If you are a dog owner who is interested in participating in these activities with your doodle, this section will provide you with valuable insights on how to train your furry companion.

First and foremost, it is crucial to understand that sporting doodle dogs are highly intelligent and trainable. They possess a natural athleticism and are eager to please their owners. This makes them ideal candidates for participating in dog sports. However, proper training is essential to harness their potential and ensure their safety.

One of the key training techniques for sporting doodle dogs is positive reinforcement. These dogs respond exceptionally well to praise, treats, and rewards. By using positive reinforcement, you can motivate and encourage your doodle to perform the desired behaviors. This can include commands such as jumping through hoops in agility or retrieving balls in flyball.

Consistency is another vital aspect of training sporting doodle dogs. Establishing a consistent routine and using the same commands will help your dog understand what is expected of them. Regular training sessions, preferably short and frequent, will help reinforce the desired behaviors and improve their skills.

It is also essential to provide mental and physical stimulation for sporting doodle dogs. Engaging them in activities that challenge their minds and bodies will keep them happy and focused. This can include setting up obstacle courses for agility training or incorporating water exercises for dock diving.

Additionally, socialization is crucial for sporting doodle dogs. Exposing them to different environments, people, and other dogs will help them become well-rounded and confident. This can be achieved through participating in training classes or joining dog sports clubs where they can interact with other dogs and handlers.

Lastly, patience and persistence are key when training sporting doodle dogs. Each dog is unique and will progress at their own pace. It is essential to remain patient and not get discouraged if your doodle faces challenges along the way. With time and dedication, they will master the skills required for dog sports.

In conclusion, training sporting doodle dogs requires a combination of positive reinforcement, consistency, mental and physical stimulation, socialization, and patience. By employing these techniques, you can unlock the full potential of your doodle and enjoy the excitement and fulfillment of participating in various dog sports and activities.

The Joys of Owning a Sporting Doodle Dog

Subchapter: The Joys of Owning a Sporting Doodle Dog

Sporting Doodle dogs, also known as active and athletic doodles, are an excellent choice for individuals who lead an active lifestyle and enjoy participating in various dog sports and activities. These doodle breeds possess the perfect combination of intelligence, agility, and energy, making them excellent companions for those who love to engage in outdoor adventures.

One of the key benefits of owning a sporting doodle dog is their natural inclination towards physical activities. Whether it's agility, flyball, or dock diving, these doodles excel in various dog sports and are always up for a challenge. Their high energy levels and athleticism allow them to perform exceptionally well in these activities, providing endless hours of fun and excitement for both dog and owner.

Furthermore, sporting doodle dogs are highly trainable and possess a strong desire to please their owners. Their intelligence and willingness to learn make them perfect candidates for obedience training and advanced commands, which are essential for participating in dog sports. With consistent training and positive reinforcement, these doodles can quickly grasp new skills and commands, impressing everyone with their abilities.

In addition to their athleticism and trainability, sporting doodle dogs also make fantastic companions for outdoor enthusiasts. Whether you enjoy hiking, running, or playing fetch in the park, these doodles will eagerly join you in your adventures. Their stamina and endurance make them ideal partners for long hikes or intense exercise sessions, ensuring that you both stay active and healthy.

Moreover, owning a sporting doodle dog promotes a healthy and active lifestyle for their owners. Regular exercise and physical activities not only benefit the dog's overall well-being but also contribute to the owner's fitness and mental health. With a sporting doodle by your side, you'll find yourself motivated to maintain an active routine and explore new outdoor activities together.

In conclusion, the joys of owning a sporting doodle dog are unparalleled for active individuals who appreciate the thrill of dog sports and outdoor adventures. These intelligent, trainable, and athletic doodles will not only impress you with their performance but also become your loyal and energetic companions. So, if you're seeking a four-legged partner to accompany you in your active lifestyle, a sporting doodle dog might be the perfect match for you.

Chapter 7: Doodle Dogs for Seniors

Factors to Consider When Choosing a Doodle Dog for Seniors

As seniors, choosing the right dog for your lifestyle is crucial for a happy and fulfilling companionship. Doodle breeds, known for their hypoallergenic and gentle nature, make excellent choices for older individuals. However, there are several factors to consider before bringing a doodle dog into your home.

Firstly, size is an essential consideration. Seniors may prefer smaller-sized doodle breeds, such as Miniature Labradoodles or Mini Goldendoodles, as they are easier to handle and require less physical exertion. These miniature doodle dogs are compact yet still possess all the wonderful qualities that make doodles so beloved.

Secondly, energy level plays a significant role in determining whether a doodle breed is suitable for seniors. Some doodles are more energetic and require regular exercise to keep them happy and healthy. For seniors who may not be as active, choosing a doodle breed with a lower energy level is recommended. Breeds like the Goldendoodle or Labradoodle are known to have a moderate energy level, making them ideal companions for seniors.

Another crucial factor to consider is trainability. Doodle breeds are highly intelligent and trainable, but some may require more effort and consistency than others. Seniors may prefer a doodle breed that is easy to train and quick to learn commands. Breeds like the Australian Labradoodle or Bernedoodle are known for their intelligence and eagerness to please, making them great choices for seniors.

Lastly, it is important to consider the grooming needs of doodle breeds. While doodles are hypoallergenic and have coats that are less likely to shed, they do require regular brushing and occasional professional grooming to prevent matting. Seniors should choose a doodle breed with a coat type that is manageable and easy to maintain. For example, a straight-coated Goldendoodle may require less grooming compared to a curly-coated Labradoodle.

In conclusion, when choosing a doodle dog for seniors, it is essential to consider factors such as size, energy level, trainability, and grooming needs. Miniature doodle breeds, moderate energy levels, easy trainability, and manageable coat types are all important factors to consider. By taking these factors into account, seniors can find the perfect doodle companion that suits their lifestyle and provides them with love, companionship, and joy in their golden years.

Doodle Breeds with Ideal Size and Energy Levels for Seniors

As we age, our needs and preferences change, and this includes the type of dog that would be the best fit for our lifestyle. For seniors looking for a furry companion, it is important to consider factors such as size, energy level, and ease of training. In this subchapter, we will explore doodle breeds that are suitable for older individuals, providing them with the perfect canine companion.

One of the main concerns for seniors is finding a dog that is the right size. Larger breeds may be too difficult to handle, while smaller breeds may not provide the companionship desired. Enter the world of miniature doodle breeds. Miniature Labradoodles and Mini Goldendoodles are smaller versions of their standard counterparts, making them easier to manage for seniors. These breeds are known for their friendly and gentle nature, making them great companions for individuals in their golden years.

Another important consideration is the energy level of the dog. Seniors may not have the same level of energy as younger individuals, so a high-energy dog may not be the best fit. Doodle breeds like the Bichonoodle or the Cavapoo are known for their moderate energy levels, striking a balance between being active and being calm. These breeds are happy to accompany their owners on leisurely walks or enjoy a relaxing day at home, making them ideal for seniors.

In addition to size and energy level, ease of training is crucial for seniors. Doodle breeds such as the Labradoodle or the Goldendoodle are intelligent and trainable, making them a great choice for older individuals. These breeds are eager to please and enjoy learning new tricks, making training sessions a fun and rewarding experience for both the dog and their owner.

For seniors who are looking for a furry companion that fits their lifestyle, doodle breeds with ideal size and energy levels are the perfect choice. Whether it's a miniature doodle breed, a moderate-energy doodle, or an intelligent and trainable doodle, there is a breed out there that will provide the perfect companionship for seniors. So, if you're a senior looking for a canine companion, consider a doodle breed that matches your needs and lifestyle – you won't be disappointed.

Training and Exercise Tips for Senior Doodle Dogs

As our beloved furry friends age, their needs and abilities change. This is especially true for senior Doodle dogs, who may require a modified training and exercise routine to ensure their health and happiness. In this subchapter, we will explore some valuable tips and techniques for training and exercising senior Doodle dogs.

1. Consider their energy level: Senior Doodle dogs may have lower energy levels compared to their younger counterparts. It is important to tailor their exercise routine accordingly. Shorter, more frequent walks or

play sessions can help keep them active without putting too much strain on their joints.

2. Focus on mental stimulation: Along with physical exercise, mental stimulation is crucial for senior Doodle dogs. Engage them in interactive games, puzzle toys, or obedience training to keep their minds sharp and prevent boredom.

3. Use positive reinforcement: Positive reinforcement is key when training senior Doodle dogs. Rewarding them with treats, praise, or playtime for good behavior will help motivate and reinforce their training efforts.

4. Be patient and gentle: As dogs age, they may experience certain physical limitations or cognitive decline. It is important to be patient and understanding during training sessions. Adjust your expectations and provide gentle guidance to help them succeed.

5. Incorporate low-impact exercises: To protect their joints and muscles, include low-impact exercises in their routine. Swimming, gentle stretching, or even short walks on soft surfaces can help keep them active without causing discomfort.

6. Regular veterinary check-ups: Senior Doodle dogs may develop age-related health issues. Regular veterinary check-ups are essential to monitor their overall health and address any concerns. Your vet can also provide guidance on appropriate exercise and training routines.

7. Adapt to their abilities: Understand that as your Doodle dog ages, their abilities may change. Be flexible and adapt your training and exercise routines to their specific needs. This may include shorter training sessions, slower-paced walks, or modified games.

By following these training and exercise tips for senior Doodle dogs, you can help ensure their physical and mental well-being in their golden years. Remember, each dog is unique, so consult with your veterinarian to create a personalized plan that suits your senior Doodle dog's specific needs.

The Companionship and Benefits of a Doodle Dog for Seniors

As we age, companionship and a furry friend to share our days with become increasingly important. For seniors looking for a loyal and loving companion, a doodle dog can be the perfect choice. Doodle breeds, such as Labradoodles or Goldendoodles, offer a unique combination of traits that make them well-suited for older individuals.

First and foremost, doodle dogs are known for their friendly and gentle nature. They have a natural affinity for people and are often very affectionate, providing unconditional love and companionship to their owners. This makes them great companions for seniors who may be living alone or looking for a constant source of companionship.

Additionally, doodles are often low-shedding and hypoallergenic, which is a major benefit for seniors with allergies. Their coats, whether curly, wavy, or straight, require regular grooming, but the lack of shedding reduces the amount of pet dander in the home, making them suitable for individuals with allergies or respiratory issues.

Size is another important consideration for seniors. Doodle breeds come in a variety of sizes, from miniature to standard, allowing seniors to choose a dog that fits their lifestyle and living arrangements. Smaller-sized doodles, such as Miniature Labradoodles or Mini Goldendoodles, are particularly well-suited for apartment living or smaller spaces.

Furthermore, doodle dogs are highly trainable and intelligent, making them ideal for seniors who may have limited physical abilities. Their eagerness to please and ability to learn commands quickly make them excellent candidates for therapy or service dog training. Doodles excel in providing emotional support and can be trained to assist with various tasks, such as retrieving items or opening doors, enhancing the independence and quality of life for seniors.

In conclusion, doodle dogs offer a multitude of benefits for seniors. Their friendly nature, hypoallergenic coats, adaptability in size, trainability, and companionship make them the perfect choice for older individuals seeking a furry friend to share their golden years with. Whether it's a Miniature Labradoodle or a Standard Goldendoodle, the companionship and benefits of a doodle dog are invaluable for seniors looking to enhance their lives with a loving and loyal companion.

Chapter 8: Doodle Dogs for Apartment Living

Doodle Breeds that Adapt Well to Apartment Living

Living in an apartment or condo doesn't mean you can't have a furry companion by your side. In fact, many doodle breeds are known for their adaptability and make excellent apartment dogs. In this subchapter, we will explore some doodle breeds that thrive in smaller living spaces, making them perfect for dog owners who reside in apartments or condos.

One popular doodle breed that adapts well to apartment living is the Miniature Labradoodle. These pint-sized pooches are a cross between a Labrador Retriever and a Miniature Poodle. Their smaller size makes them ideal for apartments, and their friendly and gentle nature makes them great companions for families with children.

Another doodle breed that is well-suited for apartment living is the Goldendoodle. These lovable dogs are a mix between a Golden Retriever and a Poodle. Goldendoodles come in various sizes, including miniatures, making them a perfect fit for smaller living spaces. With their intelligence and trainability, they can quickly learn to adapt to apartment life and thrive in a more confined environment.

If you're looking for a hypoallergenic doodle breed that is suitable for individuals with allergies, the Schnoodle is an excellent choice. This cross between a Miniature Schnauzer and a Poodle has a low-shedding coat that is less likely to trigger allergies. Their moderate energy level and small stature make them well-suited for apartment living.

For those dog owners who prefer a larger doodle breed, the Bernedoodle can still be a great option for apartment living. This mix between a Bernese Mountain Dog and a Poodle is known for its calm and gentle temperament. Despite their size, Bernedoodles are adaptable and can thrive in smaller spaces as long as they receive regular exercise and mental stimulation.

When living in an apartment, it's essential to consider the exercise requirements of your doodle breed. While they may not have a backyard to roam freely, regular walks, playtime, and mental stimulation can keep them happy and content. Additionally, providing them with puzzle toys and interactive games can help fulfill their exercise needs within the confines of your apartment.

In conclusion, if you're a dog owner living in an apartment or condo, don't fret! There are plenty of doodle breeds that adapt well to apartment living. From Miniature Labradoodles to Schnoodles, these intelligent and adaptable dogs can thrive in smaller spaces, bringing joy and companionship to their owners, even in the heart of the city.

Managing Exercise and Mental Stimulation for Apartment Doodle Dogs

Living in an apartment or a smaller space doesn't mean you can't enjoy the company of a Doodle dog. With the right approach to exercise and mental stimulation, apartment dwellers can provide a fulfilling and stimulating environment for their furry friends. In this subchapter, we will explore the strategies and activities that can keep your apartment Doodle dog happy, healthy, and entertained.

First and foremost, it is important to understand that Doodle breeds, such as Labradoodles or Goldendoodles, are known for their intelligence and high energy levels. This means they require regular exercise to keep them physically and mentally fit. However, apartment living may pose some challenges in terms of space limitations. To overcome this, consider the following activities:

1. Daily walks: Even in a smaller space, daily walks are essential for your Doodle's physical and mental well-being. Aim for at least 30 minutes to an hour of brisk walking to burn off excess energy.

2. Interactive toys: Invest in interactive toys that stimulate your dog's mind and keep them entertained. Puzzle toys or treat-dispensing toys can provide mental stimulation while keeping them occupied.

3. Indoor playtime: Create a designated space for indoor playtime, such as a playpen or a cleared-out area in your apartment. Use toys like balls or ropes for interactive play sessions.

4. Doggy daycare or playdates: Socialization is crucial for all dogs, and apartment Doodle dogs are no exception. Consider enrolling your dog in a doggy daycare program or arranging playdates with other compatible dogs in your building or neighborhood.

5. Training sessions: Doodle breeds are highly trainable, so use this to your advantage. Regular training sessions not only provide mental stimulation but also help establish a strong bond between you and your dog.

Remember, mental stimulation is just as important as physical exercise for Doodle dogs. Incorporate activities like obedience training, scent work, or agility training to keep their minds engaged and challenged.

Lastly, don't forget to provide a comfortable space for your Doodle to rest and relax. Create a cozy corner with a comfortable bed or crate where they can retreat and feel secure.

By following these strategies, you can ensure that your apartment Doodle dog leads a happy and fulfilling life, even in a smaller space. Don't let living in an apartment deter you from experiencing the joy and companionship of a Doodle breed. With the right approach, you can provide a stimulating environment that meets their exercise and mental needs.

Grooming and Maintenance for Apartment-Friendly Doodle Breeds

Living in an apartment or condo doesn't mean you have to miss out on the joy of owning a doodle dog. With their friendly nature and adaptable personalities, many doodle breeds can thrive in smaller living spaces. However, it's important to understand that these breeds still require regular grooming and maintenance to keep them happy and healthy.

One of the key factors to consider when choosing a doodle breed for apartment living is their size. Miniature doodles, such as Miniature Labradoodles or Mini Goldendoodles, are ideal for smaller spaces. Their compact size allows them to comfortably navigate tight hallways and confined living areas without feeling cramped.

When it comes to grooming, doodle breeds with wavy or curly coats, like the Labradoodle or Goldendoodle, require regular brushing to prevent matting and tangling. It's recommended to brush their coats at least once a week, using a slicker brush or a comb with wide, rounded teeth. This will help to remove loose hair and prevent their coats from becoming matted.

Bathing is another important aspect of grooming for apartment-friendly doodle breeds. It's recommended to bathe them every 4-6 weeks, using a gentle dog shampoo that won't strip their coats of natural oils. Be sure to thoroughly rinse their coats to remove all shampoo residue, as any leftover product can cause skin irritation.

Trimming their nails regularly is also crucial for their comfort and overall well-being. Long nails can be uncomfortable for doodles, especially in smaller living spaces where they may not have as much opportunity to wear them down naturally. Use a high-quality nail trimmer designed for dogs, and be careful not to cut the quick.

Lastly, don't forget about dental care. Doodle breeds, like many other dogs, are prone to dental issues such as tartar buildup and gum disease. Brush their teeth regularly with a dog-friendly toothbrush and toothpaste to maintain good oral hygiene.

Living in an apartment shouldn't deter you from owning a doodle dog. With proper grooming and maintenance, these lovable breeds can thrive in smaller living spaces. So, if you're considering bringing a doodle into your apartment, make sure to prioritize their grooming needs to keep them looking and feeling their best.

Creating a Harmonious Living Environment with an Apartment Doodle Dog

Living in an apartment or condo doesn't mean you have to give up on your dream of having a dog. With the right breed, you can create a harmonious living environment that suits both you and your furry friend. If you're considering a doodle dog and live in a smaller space, this sub-niche is perfect for you.

Doodle breeds, such as the Miniature Labradoodles or Mini Goldendoodles, are known for their adaptability and size, making them ideal companions for apartment living. These smaller-sized doodles are not only adorable but also have lower exercise requirements compared to their larger counterparts.

One of the key factors to consider when living in an apartment with a doodle dog is their exercise needs. While they may not require extensive outdoor space, they still need regular physical activity to keep them happy and healthy. Daily walks, trips to the dog park, or playdates with other dogs can help meet their exercise requirements.

Another aspect to consider is their temperament. Doodle breeds are known for their friendly and gentle nature, making them great companions for families with children or older individuals. Their intelligence and trainable nature also make them suitable for apartment living, as they can be easily taught proper behavior and house manners.

Additionally, doodle breeds are often hypoallergenic, which is a significant benefit for individuals with allergies. Their low-shedding coats produce fewer allergens, making them a suitable choice for allergy sufferers who want a dog in their apartment.

When living in an apartment with a doodle dog, it's also essential to create a designated space for them. Providing a comfortable bed or crate, as well as toys and enrichment activities, can help keep them entertained and prevent destructive behaviors. Regular grooming is also necessary to maintain their coat's health and prevent matting.

In conclusion, choosing a doodle breed that adapts well to apartment living can create a harmonious environment for both you and your dog. Their smaller size, hypoallergenic coats, friendly nature, and lower exercise requirements make them ideal companions for individuals living in apartments or condos. With proper care, training, and attention to their needs, you can enjoy the company of your doodle dog in your apartment and create a loving and harmonious living environment.

Chapter 9: Doodle Dogs with Unique Coat Colors

Rare and Unique Coat Colors in Doodle Breeds

When it comes to doodle breeds, one of the many reasons why they are so popular among dog owners is their unique and eye-catching coat colors. While doodles are already known for their hypoallergenic and low-shedding coats, some breeds take it a step further by offering rare and unique coat colors that are sure to turn heads. In this subchapter, we will dive into the world of doodle breeds with rare and unique coat colors, such as merle, phantom, and parti-color variations.

Merle coats, characterized by a marbled or swirled pattern of colors, are highly sought after by dog owners looking for something truly unique. Breeds like the Australian Labradoodle and the Bernedoodle often come in stunning merle variations, featuring a combination of different shades and hues. These coats are not only visually striking but also add an extra layer of charm to these already adorable doodle breeds.

Phantom coats, on the other hand, are characterized by two distinct colors, with one color being more prominent on specific areas of the body. Typically, the darker color appears on the body, while the lighter color can be seen on the eyebrows, muzzle, and legs. Breeds like the Goldendoodle and the Cockapoo often come in phantom variations, adding a touch of elegance and sophistication to their already lovable appearance.

Parti-color coats, also known as piebald coats, are a true testament to the diversity and uniqueness of doodle breeds. These coats feature large patches of two or more colors, creating a beautiful mosaic-like pattern. Doodle breeds like the Labradoodle and the Sheepadoodle often come in parti-color variations, offering a truly one-of-a-kind look that is sure to make any dog owner proud.

Whether you're looking for a doodle breed with a merle, phantom, or parti-color coat, it's important to note that these unique coat colors often come with a higher price tag. Additionally, these coat colors may also require extra grooming and care to maintain their vibrancy and beauty.

In conclusion, if you're a dog owner who appreciates rarity and uniqueness, doodle breeds with rare and unique coat colors are the perfect choice for you. From the mesmerizing merle coats to the sophisticated phantom variations and the striking parti-color patterns, these breeds are sure to stand out in any crowd. So if you're ready to add a touch of individuality to your furry family member, consider a doodle breed with a rare and unique coat color.

Merle Doodle Dogs: Characteristics and Care

Merle Doodle dogs are a unique and stunning type of doodle breed that stands out for its striking coat pattern. In this subchapter, we will explore the characteristics and care of Merle Doodle dogs, catering to dog owners who are interested in this specific coat color variation.

Merle Doodle dogs are known for their beautiful coat colors, which can range from a mix of blue, black, and gray to a combination of red, brown, and cream. The merle pattern creates a marbled or mottled effect, giving these dogs a truly eye-catching appearance. However, it's important to note that the Merle gene can also be associated with certain health concerns, such as deafness or vision problems. Therefore, it is crucial for dog owners to obtain Merle Doodle puppies from reputable breeders who prioritize the health and well-being of their dogs.

In terms of care, Merle Doodle dogs require regular grooming to maintain their luxurious coats. The specific grooming needs may vary depending on the doodle breed they belong to, such as Labradoodles or Goldendoodles. However, in general, Merle Doodle dogs should be brushed regularly to prevent matting and tangling. They may also require occasional trimming or professional grooming to keep their coats in top condition. Additionally, routine ear cleaning, teeth brushing, and nail trimming are essential parts of their overall care.

Merle Doodle dogs are not only visually stunning but also known for their friendly and gentle nature, making them great companions for families with children. They are intelligent and trainable, which also makes them suitable candidates for service or therapy dog training. However, it is important to note that their energy levels can vary depending on the specific doodle breed, so it's important for owners to provide them with enough exercise and mental stimulation to keep them happy and healthy.

In conclusion, Merle Doodle dogs are a captivating and unique choice for dog owners who are drawn to their distinctive coat colors. However, it is crucial to prioritize the health and well-being of these dogs by obtaining them from reputable breeders and providing them with proper care and grooming. With their friendly and gentle nature, Merle Doodle dogs can make excellent companions for families, individuals with allergies, or anyone looking for a special addition to their household.

Phantom and Parti-Color Doodle Dogs: Traits and Training

In the vast world of Doodle dogs, there are numerous breeds and variations to choose from. One unique sub-niche within this realm is Phantom and Parti-Color Doodle dogs. These breeds stand out from the crowd due to their rare and striking coat colors, making them a popular choice for dog owners seeking something eye-catching and extraordinary.

Phantom and Parti-Color Doodle dogs possess a coat pattern that includes two or more distinct colors. The Phantom pattern typically consists of a solid base color with markings of a second color on specific areas of the body, such as the face, paws, or legs. On the other hand, Parti-Color Doodle dogs have a coat that is predominantly white with patches or spots of one or more colors. These unique coat patterns make Phantom and Parti-Color Doodle dogs a visual delight for both their owners and passersby.

Aside from their distinctive looks, Phantom and Parti-Color Doodle dogs also boast other desirable traits that make them excellent companions. They are known for their friendly and gentle nature, making them ideal for families with children or individuals seeking a loving and loyal pet. Additionally, these breeds are highly intelligent and trainable, which makes them suitable for service or therapy dog roles. Their calm temperament and willingness to please make them a natural fit for these types of specialized training.

However, it's important to note that owning a Phantom or Parti-Color Doodle dog also comes with its own set of considerations. Their unique coat colors may require extra grooming and maintenance to keep them looking their best. Regular brushing and occasional professional grooming may be necessary to prevent matting and keep their coats healthy and vibrant.

When it comes to training, Phantom and Parti-Color Doodle dogs respond well to positive reinforcement methods. They are eager to please their owners, which makes training sessions enjoyable and rewarding for both parties. Consistency and patience are key when training these intelligent breeds, and early socialization is essential to ensure they grow up to be well-rounded and confident dogs.

In conclusion, Phantom and Parti-Color Doodle dogs bring a touch of uniqueness and beauty to the world of Doodle breeds. Their rare and stunning coat colors, combined with their friendly nature and trainability, make them an excellent choice for dog owners looking for something special. Whether you're seeking a family companion, a therapy dog, or simply a furry friend with a striking appearance, these breeds are sure to capture your heart and bring joy to your life.

The Appeal of Doodle Dogs with Uncommon Coat Colors

When it comes to doodle dogs, their charming personalities and hypoallergenic coats have made them a popular choice among dog owners. However, there is one aspect of doodle dogs that adds an extra touch of uniqueness: their coat colors. While most people are familiar with the traditional solid colors of doodle breeds, there are some doodles that boast rare or uncommon coat colors, making them stand out from the crowd.

For dog owners who want a doodle with a coat that is truly eye-catching, breeds like the merle, phantom, or parti-color variations are perfect choices. Merle doodles have a fascinating coat pattern with a mix of colors, creating a marbled effect that is simply stunning. Phantom doodles feature two colors, usually black and a lighter shade, with distinct markings that give them an elegant and sophisticated appearance. Parti-color doodles, on the other hand, have a coat that is predominantly white with patches of another color, resulting in a playful and lively look.

These uncommon coat colors not only make doodle dogs visually appealing but also allow owners to express their individuality. Whether you're looking for a doodle that matches your unique style or simply want a dog that stands out in a crowd, these uncommon coat colors are sure to turn heads and spark conversations.

In addition to their striking appearance, doodles with uncommon coat colors still possess all the wonderful qualities that make doodles so beloved. They are known for their friendly and gentle nature, making them great companions for families with children. They also excel in various dog sports and activities, thanks to their intelligence and athleticism. Moreover, doodles with rare coat colors can still be hypoallergenic, making them suitable for individuals with allergies.

If you're a dog owner who enjoys the beauty of uncommon coat colors and wants a doodle that is both visually stunning and has a wonderful temperament, consider exploring the world of doodles with unique coat colors. These dogs not only bring joy and companionship but also add a touch of uniqueness to your life. So why settle for ordinary when you can have a doodle with an extraordinary coat color?

Chapter 10: Doodle Dogs with Specific Coat Types

Understanding Different Coat Types in Doodle Breeds

When it comes to doodle dogs, one of the most fascinating aspects is their unique coat types. Whether you're looking for a hypoallergenic breed, a smaller-sized companion, a family-friendly pet, or a sporting partner, understanding the various coat types can help you choose the perfect doodle for your needs.

For allergy sufferers, hypoallergenic doodle breeds are a popular choice. These dogs have hair instead of fur, which reduces the amount of allergens they produce. Breeds such as the Labradoodle and Goldendoodle often have curly or wavy coats that require regular grooming to prevent matting and keep them hypoallergenic.

Miniature doodle dogs are perfect for those seeking a smaller-sized companion. Miniature Labradoodles and Mini Goldendoodles are adorable, compact versions of their standard counterparts. Their coats can vary from curly to straight, but they all require regular grooming to maintain their appearance and prevent matting.

Families with children often seek doodle breeds known for their friendly and gentle nature. Breeds like the Australian Labradoodle and Bernedoodle are great choices for families as they are patient, loyal, and love to play. Their coats can be curly, wavy, or straight, offering a variety of options to suit different preferences.

For those in need of service or therapy dogs, doodle breeds are a popular choice due to their intelligence, trainability, and temperament. Whether it's a curly-coated Labradoodle or a wavy-coated Goldendoodle, these breeds excel in assisting individuals with disabilities or providing emotional support.

If you're into dog sports and activities, sporting doodle breeds are worth considering. With their high energy levels and athleticism, breeds like the Sheepadoodle and Aussiedoodle are perfect companions for agility, flyball, or even dock diving. Their coats can range from curly to straight, but regular grooming is essential to keep them looking their best.

Seniors looking for a suitable doodle breed should consider factors like size, energy level, and ease of training. Smaller doodle breeds like the Cavapoo or Cockapoo are often a good fit for older individuals. Their coats can be curly or wavy, providing a soft and low-maintenance option.

Living in smaller spaces like apartments or condos doesn't mean you can't have a doodle companion. Doodle breeds like the Whoodle or Labradoodle are adaptable to apartment living due to their size and exercise requirements. Their coats can be curly, wavy, or straight, depending on your preference.

For those who appreciate unique coat colors, doodle breeds offer a variety of options. From merle to phantom and parti-color variations, breeds like the Bernedoodle or Aussiedoodle can add a touch of uniqueness to your family.

Lastly, if you lead an active lifestyle and enjoy outdoor activities like hiking or running, there are doodle breeds that are perfect companions. With their high energy levels and athleticism, breeds like the Goldendoodle or Labradoodle are excellent choices. Their coats can be curly, wavy, or straight, but regular grooming is essential to keep them comfortable during outdoor adventures.

Understanding the different coat types in doodle breeds is crucial in finding the perfect companion for your lifestyle. Whether you have allergies, live in a small space, or have specific preferences, there is a doodle breed out there that will fit your needs. So, dive into the world of doodle dogs and find the perfect furry friend for you!

Curly-Coated Doodle Dogs: Grooming and Maintenance

When it comes to doodle dogs with curly coats, proper grooming and maintenance are essential to keep their fur looking its best. Whether you have a Labradoodle, Goldendoodle, or any other curly-coated doodle breed, understanding the unique needs of their coats will help you keep them healthy and happy.

Curly coats require regular brushing to prevent matting and tangling. Using a slicker brush or a comb with wide-spaced teeth, gently brush through your dog's fur, starting from the roots and working your way to the tips. This will help remove any loose hair and prevent matting. It is recommended to brush your doodle dog at least two to three times a week, but daily brushing is even better for preventing tangles.

In addition to regular brushing, curly-coated doodles may also require professional grooming. This includes regular haircuts to maintain their coat's length and prevent it from becoming too unruly. Professional groomers are experienced in working with curly coats and can trim your dog's fur in a way that suits their breed's specific requirements.

Bathing your curly-coated doodle dog is also an important part of their grooming routine. Use a mild dog shampoo and ensure you thoroughly rinse out all the shampoo from their fur. After bathing, it is crucial to dry their coat completely, as damp fur can lead to skin irritations and unpleasant odors. Use a towel to remove excess moisture and consider using a blow dryer on a low heat setting to ensure their coat is completely dry.

Regular trips to the groomer also provide an opportunity to check your dog's ears, eyes, and teeth for any signs of infection or other issues. Ear infections can be common in dogs with curly coats due to the trapped moisture, so it is important to keep their ears clean and dry.

By following these grooming and maintenance tips, you can help your curly-coated doodle dog maintain a healthy and beautiful coat. Remember, regular brushing, professional grooming, and proper bathing techniques are key to keeping their curly fur in top condition. Your doodle dog will thank you for the extra care and attention you give to their unique coat type.

Wavy-Coated Doodle Dogs: Care and Styling

When it comes to Doodle dogs with wavy coats, their unique fur requires special care and attention. In this subchapter, we will explore the care and styling needs of wavy-coated Doodle dogs, providing valuable information for dog owners who have chosen these breeds as their beloved companions.

Caring for a wavy-coated Doodle dog starts with regular grooming. The wavy coat is prone to matting and tangling, so daily brushing is essential to keep it in top condition. Use a slicker brush or a comb with wide-spaced teeth to gently remove any tangles and prevent matting. Regular bathing with a high-quality dog shampoo is also important to maintain the coat's health and shine.

When it comes to styling wavy-coated Doodle dogs, there are several options to consider. Many owners prefer to keep their dog's coat long and flowing, which requires regular trims to keep it at a manageable length. Professional grooming services can help you achieve the desired look, whether it's a classic teddy bear cut or a more natural, tousled appearance.

For those who prefer a shorter coat, a puppy cut or a sporty trim may be more suitable. These styles not only make grooming easier but also give your wavy-coated Doodle dog a fresh and youthful look.

In addition to grooming and styling, it's crucial to provide proper nutrition and exercise for your wavy-coated Doodle dog. A balanced diet rich in essential nutrients will promote a healthy coat and overall well-being. Regular exercise, such as daily walks or playtime in a fenced yard, will help keep your dog physically fit and mentally stimulated.

For individuals with allergies, wavy-coated Doodle dogs can be a great choice. Their hypoallergenic coats produce minimal dander, making them less likely to trigger allergic reactions. However, it's important to note that individual allergies may vary, so it's always recommended to spend time with a specific breed before bringing one home.

In conclusion, wavy-coated Doodle dogs require special care and styling to keep their unique fur in optimal condition. Regular grooming, proper nutrition, and exercise are vital for maintaining their health and well-being. Whether you choose a longer or shorter coat style, wavy-coated Doodle dogs are sure to bring joy and companionship to dog owners in various niches, including allergy sufferers, families with children, and active individuals seeking a furry partner for outdoor adventures.

Straight-Coated Doodle Dogs: Tips for Coat Care

If you are a dog owner who has a straight-coated doodle dog, it's important to understand the unique needs of their coat. Straight-coated doodle breeds, such as the Straight Labradoodle or Straight Goldendoodle, have a different coat texture than their curly or wavy counterparts. In this subchapter, we will provide you with some valuable tips for coat care to keep your straight-coated doodle looking and feeling their best.

1. Regular Brushing: Straight-coated doodles require regular brushing to prevent matting and tangling. Use a slicker brush or a combination brush to gently remove any tangles or loose hair from their coat. Aim to brush them at least once a week to maintain a healthy and shiny coat.

2. Bathing: Straight-coated doodles can be bathed every 4-6 weeks, depending on their activity level and how dirty they get. Use a dog-specific shampoo and conditioner to keep their coat clean and moisturized. Be sure to thoroughly rinse out all the products to avoid any residue.

3. Drying: After bathing, make sure to dry your straight-coated doodle thoroughly. Use a towel to remove excess moisture, and then use a blow dryer on a low heat setting. Avoid using high heat as it can damage their coat. Brush their coat while drying to prevent any tangles from forming.

4. Trimming: While straight-coated doodles don't require extensive grooming like their curly or wavy counterparts, regular trimming is still necessary to keep their coat neat and tidy. Trim the hair around their face, ears, and paws to maintain a well-groomed appearance.

5. Regular Maintenance: In addition to brushing and trimming, it's essential to check your straight-coated doodle's ears, eyes, and nails regularly. Clean their ears with a dog-specific ear cleaner, trim their nails as needed, and check their eyes for any signs of irritation or infection.

By following these coat care tips, you can ensure that your straight-coated doodle dog looks and feels their best. Remember to establish a grooming routine early on to help them become comfortable with the process. With proper care and attention, your straight-coated doodle can have a healthy and beautiful coat that will make heads turn wherever you go.

Choosing the Right Coat Type for Your Doodle Dog

When it comes to doodle dogs, one of the most distinctive features is their unique coat. Doodle breeds, such as Labradoodles and Goldendoodles, come in a variety of coat types, including curly, wavy, and straight. As a dog owner, it's essential to understand the different coat types and choose the one that suits your needs and preferences.

For dog owners who are allergy sufferers, hypoallergenic doodle breeds are an excellent choice. These breeds have minimal shedding and produce fewer allergens, making them more suitable for individuals with allergies. Look for doodle breeds with curly or wavy coats, as they tend to be hypoallergenic.

If you're looking for a smaller-sized doodle dog, consider miniature doodle breeds. These adorable pups, such as Miniature Labradoodles or Mini Goldendoodles, are perfect for those who prefer a compact companion. Miniature doodles usually have a curly or wavy coat, which adds to their charm.

For families with children, doodle breeds known for their friendly and gentle nature are ideal. These breeds make great companions for kids, and their hypoallergenic coats are an added bonus. Look for doodle breeds with curly or wavy coats, as they tend to be more patient and tolerant.

If you're considering a doodle dog as a service or therapy dog, certain breeds are more suitable due to their intelligence, trainability, and temperament. Look for doodle breeds with curly or wavy coats, as they are often highly trainable and have a calm and gentle demeanor.

For individuals with active lifestyles, doodle breeds that excel in various dog sports and activities are a perfect match. These athletic dogs enjoy outdoor activities like hiking, running, and agility. Look for doodle breeds with wavy or straight coats, as they tend to have a more streamlined physique for optimal performance.

For seniors or individuals living in smaller spaces like apartments, doodle breeds that adapt well to these conditions are a great choice. Look for smaller-sized doodle breeds with curly or wavy coats, as they are usually more adaptable and have lower exercise requirements.

Lastly, for those seeking a doodle dog with a unique appearance, breeds with rare or unique coat colors are worth considering. Look for doodle breeds with merle, phantom, or parti-color variations to add a touch of uniqueness to your furry companion.

In conclusion, when choosing the right coat type for your doodle dog, consider your specific needs and preferences. Whether you're an allergy sufferer, have a family with children, or lead an active lifestyle, there is a doodle breed with the perfect coat type for you. Take the time to research and understand the different coat types to ensure a happy and harmonious relationship with your doodle dog.

Chapter 11: Doodle Dogs for Active Lifestyles

Doodle Breeds Known for Their High Energy Levels

When it comes to choosing a furry companion, energy levels play a crucial role in determining the right fit for your lifestyle. For dog owners with an active lifestyle or those looking for a four-legged exercise buddy, certain doodle breeds are renowned for their high energy levels. In this subchapter, we will explore doodle breeds that are perfect for individuals with active lifestyles.

1. Goldendoodle: This popular doodle breed combines the intelligence and athleticism of a Golden Retriever with the low-shedding coat of a Poodle. Goldendoodles love outdoor activities like hiking, swimming, and running, making them an ideal choice for active individuals.

2. Labradoodle: Known for their outgoing and energetic nature, Labradoodles are a mix of a Labrador Retriever and a Poodle. With their high intelligence and willingness to please, they excel in activities like agility, flyball, and dock diving.

3. Aussiedoodle: This energetic doodle breed is a mix of an Australian Shepherd and a Poodle. Aussiedoodles are highly intelligent and require mental and physical stimulation to thrive. They are excellent candidates for dog sports and outdoor adventures.

4. Bernedoodle: Combining the playful nature of a Bernese Mountain Dog with the intelligence of a Poodle, Bernedoodles are known for their boundless energy. They thrive in active households and enjoy activities like hiking, jogging, and playing fetch.

5. Sheepadoodle: A cross between a Old English Sheepdog and a Poodle, Sheepadoodles possess a fun-loving and energetic personality. They

require regular exercise to keep their energy levels in check and enjoy activities like obedience training and agility.

These high-energy doodle breeds are perfect for individuals who lead an active lifestyle and enjoy outdoor adventures. However, it's important to note that their energy levels need to be properly channeled through physical exercise and mental stimulation. Failing to meet their energy requirements may result in behavioral issues. If you're considering one of these breeds, ensure that you have the time, dedication, and resources to provide them with the exercise and mental stimulation they need to thrive.

In the next subchapter, we will explore doodle breeds suitable for individuals living in smaller spaces, such as apartments or condos. Stay tuned to find the perfect doodle breed for your living situation!

Engaging Activities for Active Doodle Dogs

If you are a dog owner with an active lifestyle, you know how important it is to keep your furry friend entertained and engaged. Doodle dogs, with their intelligence and playful nature, are the perfect companions for those who lead an active lifestyle. In this subchapter, we will explore some engaging activities specifically tailored for active doodle dogs.

First and foremost, doodle dogs love to play fetch. This classic game is not only a great way to exercise your dog, but it also helps strengthen the bond between you and your furry friend. Whether you're throwing a ball in the park or using a Frisbee, your doodle will have a blast chasing after it.

Another activity that doodle dogs excel in is agility training. These dogs are known for their athleticism and quick learning abilities, making them perfect candidates for agility courses. Set up a small course in your backyard or join a local agility club to challenge your doodle's physical and mental abilities.

For water-loving doodles, swimming is an excellent activity to keep them active and cool during the summer months. Take your doodle to a dog-friendly beach or invest in a kiddie pool for your backyard. Not only will your furry friend get a great workout, but swimming is also gentle on their joints.

If you're an avid hiker or runner, consider taking your doodle along on your outdoor adventures. Doodle dogs, with their high energy levels, thrive in environments where they can burn off their excess energy. Before embarking on any strenuous activities, make sure to consult with your veterinarian to ensure your doodle is in good physical condition.

Lastly, mental stimulation is just as important as physical exercise for active doodle dogs. Engage their minds by teaching them new tricks or participating in obedience training classes. These activities not only keep your doodle mentally stimulated but also strengthen the bond between you and your furry friend.

In conclusion, doodle dogs are perfect companions for those with active lifestyles. Whether you're playing fetch, participating in agility training, swimming, hiking, or engaging in mental stimulation activities, your doodle will thrive in an environment that challenges them physically and mentally. Remember to always prioritize your dog's safety and consult with your veterinarian before embarking on any strenuous activities. Enjoy your adventures with your active doodle!

Training and Exercise Regimens for Active Doodle Owners

If you're an active individual who loves outdoor activities like hiking, running, or simply staying active, and you also happen to be a proud doodle owner, you're in luck! Doodle breeds are known for their high energy levels and athleticism, making them the perfect companions for those with an active lifestyle. In this subchapter, we will explore the training and exercise regimens that are best suited for active doodle owners.

When it comes to training your active doodle, consistency and positive reinforcement are key. Doodles are intelligent and trainable dogs, so it's important to provide them with mental stimulation and challenges. Consider enrolling in obedience classes or hiring a professional trainer to help you and your doodle master basic commands and advanced tricks. These training sessions not only provide mental stimulation but also strengthen the bond between you and your furry friend.

In addition to training, regular exercise is crucial for keeping your active doodle happy and healthy. Doodles thrive in environments where they can burn off their energy, so make sure to incorporate daily exercise into their routine. This can include long walks, jogging, hiking, or even playing fetch in a fenced yard. If you have access to a dog park, take advantage of it! Doodles love socializing with other dogs, and it's a great way for them to release their energy in a safe and controlled environment.

To keep your active doodle engaged during exercise, consider incorporating activities that tap into their natural instincts. For example, agility training can help them improve their coordination and problem-solving skills while also providing a great physical workout. Other activities like flyball or dock diving can be fun and exciting for both you and your doodle.

Remember, each doodle is unique, and their exercise needs may vary. Factors such as age, size, and overall health should be taken into consideration when designing their exercise regimen. Always consult with your veterinarian to ensure that your doodle's exercise routine is safe and appropriate for their specific needs.

In conclusion, if you lead an active lifestyle and are considering adding a furry companion to your adventures, a doodle breed may be the perfect fit. With their high energy levels and athleticism, doodles are well-suited for active individuals who enjoy outdoor activities. By providing consistent training and incorporating regular exercise into their routine, you and your doodle can enjoy an active and fulfilling life together.

The Rewards of Owning an Active Doodle Dog

If you're an active individual who enjoys outdoor activities like hiking, running, or even just long walks in the park, owning an active doodle dog can be incredibly rewarding. These energetic and athletic breeds are the perfect companions for those who lead an active lifestyle. In this subchapter, we will explore why owning an active doodle dog can bring so many rewards to dog owners like yourself.

Active doodle dogs, such as the Goldendoodle or Labradoodle, are known for their high energy levels and love for physical exercise. They thrive on regular exercise and are always up for a good adventure. Whether it's going for a jog in the morning or playing fetch in the backyard, these dogs will keep you motivated and active.

One of the main rewards of owning an active doodle dog is the opportunity to bond with your furry friend while engaging in physical activities. Spending quality time outdoors with your dog not only improves your physical health but also strengthens the emotional bond between you and your pet. The shared experiences and adventures create lasting memories that you will cherish for a lifetime.

In addition to the physical benefits, owning an active doodle dog can also have a positive impact on your mental well-being. Regular exercise has been proven to reduce stress, anxiety, and depression. Having a companion who encourages and motivates you to stay active can greatly improve your overall mood and mental health.

Furthermore, active doodle dogs are highly intelligent and trainable, making them excellent candidates for various dog sports and activities. Whether it's agility, flyball, or dock diving, these breeds excel in competitive sports and are always eager to learn new tricks. Participating in these activities not only provides mental stimulation for your dog but also allows you to showcase their talents and abilities.

Lastly, owning an active doodle dog can lead to a healthier and more active lifestyle for you as well. These dogs require regular exercise, which means you will be more motivated to stay active and fit. They will encourage you to get outdoors and explore new places, helping you maintain a healthy weight and improve your cardiovascular health.

In conclusion, owning an active doodle dog can bring numerous rewards to dog owners who lead an active lifestyle. From the opportunity to bond and create lasting memories, to the positive impact on your mental well-being, these energetic and athletic breeds offer so much more than just a furry companion. So if you're someone who loves staying active and enjoys outdoor adventures, an active doodle dog may be the perfect addition to your family.

Conclusion: Finding the Perfect Doodle Dog for You

In this book, we have explored the various coat types of doodle dogs and how they can cater to the specific needs and preferences of dog owners. Whether you are an allergy sufferer, a family with children, a senior, or someone with an active lifestyle, there is a doodle dog out there that is perfect for you.

For allergy sufferers, doodle breeds that are hypoallergenic and have minimal shedding are the ideal choice. These breeds, such as the Labradoodle or Goldendoodle, have a mix of poodle genes, which means they produce less dander and allergens.

If you are looking for a smaller-sized doodle dog, miniature breeds like the Miniature Labradoodle or Mini Goldendoodle are the perfect fit. They still possess the same lovable and friendly nature as their larger counterparts but require less space and exercise.

Families with children need a dog that is gentle, friendly, and patient. Doodle breeds like the Goldendoodle or Bernedoodle are known for their gentle temperament and make great companions for kids. They are also highly trainable, making them suitable for families looking for a well-behaved dog.

Service and therapy dogs play an important role in helping individuals with disabilities or emotional support needs. Doodle breeds like the Labradoodle or Australian Labradoodle are known for their intelligence, trainability, and calm temperament, making them excellent candidates for service or therapy work.

For those who enjoy participating in dog sports and activities, sporting doodle breeds are the way to go. These breeds, such as the Australian Labradoodle or Bernedoodle, excel in agility, flyball, and other dog sports due to their athleticism and high energy levels.

Seniors need a dog that is easy to handle, low maintenance, and suitable for their lifestyle. Doodle breeds like the Cavapoo or Shihpoo are small in size, have a moderate energy level, and are easy to train, making them the perfect companion for older individuals.

If you live in an apartment or condo, a doodle breed that adapts well to smaller spaces is essential. Breeds like the Cockapoo or Maltipoo are small in size and have lower exercise requirements, making them suitable for apartment living.

For those who appreciate unique coat colors, doodle breeds like the Merle Labradoodle or Phantom Goldendoodle offer a wide range of rare and unique coat variations that will surely turn heads wherever you go.

Lastly, for individuals with specific coat preferences, doodle breeds with curly, wavy, or straight coats provide options for those who have a preference for a particular coat type.

No matter what your lifestyle or preferences may be, there is a doodle dog that is perfect for you. By considering the sub-niches discussed in this book, you can find the ideal companion that will bring joy, love, and happiness to your life. Happy doodle dog hunting!

Resources for Further Information

As a dog owner, it's important to have access to reliable information about your furry friend, especially when it comes to specific niches within the world of doodle dogs. Whether you're looking for a hypoallergenic breed, a smaller-sized companion, or a doodle suitable for families with children, this subchapter provides a list of resources to help you further explore these topics.

1. Allergy-Friendly Doodle Breeds:

- "The Ultimate Guide to Hypoallergenic Doodle Breeds" by Dr. Sarah Thompson: This comprehensive guide discusses the different hypoallergenic doodle breeds, their coat types, and tips for managing allergies.

- "Living with Allergies and a Doodle Dog" by Allergy-Free Paws: This website specializes in providing information and resources for dog owners with allergies, including a list of hypoallergenic doodle breeds.

2. Miniature Doodle Breeds:

- "Miniature Doodle Dogs: The Perfect Size for Any Home" by DoodleLovers.com: This article explores the characteristics and care requirements of various miniature doodle breeds, helping you make an informed decision based on your living situation and preferences.

- "Miniature Doodle Breeders Directory" by MiniDoodle.com: This directory provides a list of reputable breeders specializing in miniature doodle breeds, ensuring you find a responsible source for your new companion.

3. Doodle Breeds for Families with Children:

- "The Best Doodle Dogs for Families" by DoodleFamily.com: This resource highlights doodle breeds known for their friendly and gentle nature, making them ideal companions for families with kids.

- "Raising a Doodle Dog: A Guide for Families" by the Doodle Dog Club: This book offers tips and advice on raising a doodle in a family environment, including training, socialization, and safety.

4. Service and Therapy Doodle Breeds:

- "The Intelligent Doodle: A Guide to Service and Therapy Dog Breeds" by ServiceDoodles.com: This guide explores the qualities and characteristics that make certain doodle breeds well-suited for service and therapy work, including their intelligence, trainability, and temperament.

- "Training Your Doodle as a Therapy Dog" by TherapyDoodle.org: This website provides resources and training tips specifically tailored to doodle owners interested in pursuing therapy dog certification.

These resources should serve as a starting point for dog owners interested in specific niches within the world of doodle dogs. Remember to always do thorough research and consult with reputable breeders or professionals before making any decisions about adding a new furry family member to your home.

Glossary of Terms

In order to fully understand the world of doodle dogs and make informed decisions about which breed is right for you, it's essential to familiarize yourself with some key terms. This glossary will serve as a helpful reference, providing definitions for terms commonly used when discussing different aspects of doodle dogs.

1. Hypoallergenic: Refers to doodle breeds that are less likely to cause allergic reactions in individuals with allergies. These breeds typically have hair rather than fur and shed less dander.

2. Miniature: Denotes smaller-sized doodle breeds, such as Miniature Labradoodles or Mini Goldendoodles. These dogs are perfect for those seeking a compact companion.

3. Family-friendly: Describes doodle breeds known for their friendly and gentle nature, making them great companions for families with children. These dogs are patient, loving, and tolerant.

4. Service and therapy dogs: Doodle breeds that are commonly trained to assist individuals with disabilities or provide emotional support. These dogs are highly intelligent, trainable, and possess a calm temperament.

5. Sporting: Refers to doodle breeds that excel in various dog sports and activities, such as agility, flyball, or dock diving. These dogs are highly athletic and enjoy being active participants.

6. Senior-friendly: Denotes doodle breeds that are suitable for older individuals. Factors such as size, energy level, and ease of training are considered when selecting breeds for seniors.

7. Apartment living: Describes doodle breeds that adapt well to living in smaller spaces, such as apartments or condos. These breeds have lower exercise requirements and are generally more calm and relaxed.

8. Unique coat colors: Refers to doodle breeds with rare or unique coat colors, such as merle, phantom, or parti-color variations. These dogs often stand out and attract attention due to their striking appearances.

9. Specific coat types: Denotes doodle breeds with specific coat types, such as curly, wavy, or straight. This category caters to individuals with specific preferences for the type of coat they desire in a dog.

10. Active lifestyles: Describes doodle breeds that are known for their high energy levels and athleticism, making them suitable for active individuals who enjoy outdoor activities like hiking or running. These dogs thrive in environments that provide plenty of exercise opportunities.

By familiarizing yourself with these terms, you'll be better equipped to navigate the diverse world of doodle dogs and find the perfect companion that fits your specific needs and preferences. Whether you're looking for a hypoallergenic breed, a companion for your family, or a sporting partner, understanding these terms will aid you in making an informed decision.

Acknowledgments

I would like to take a moment to express my deepest gratitude to all those who have contributed to the creation of this book. Without their support, expertise, and unwavering dedication, "Curly, Wavy, or Straight: Unraveling the Coat Types of Doodle Dogs for Dog Owners" would not have been possible.

First and foremost, I would like to thank the dog owners who have shared their experiences and insights with us. Your love for your furry companions and your commitment to their well-being have served as the inspiration for this book. Your stories and anecdotes have provided invaluable information and guidance for fellow dog owners, especially those within specific niches.

To the dog owners in the sub-niche of doodle dogs for allergy sufferers, your knowledge about hypoallergenic breeds and their suitability for individuals with allergies has been greatly appreciated. Your expertise has helped us shed light on the best doodle breeds for those seeking a canine companion without the added allergy concerns.

A special thank you goes out to the dog owners in the sub-niche of miniature doodle dogs. Your insights into smaller-sized doodle breeds, such as Miniature Labradoodles and Mini Goldendoodles, have allowed us to provide tailored advice for those seeking a pint-sized doodle companion.

To the dog owners in the sub-niche of doodle dogs for families with children, your stories about the friendly and gentle nature of these breeds have been invaluable. Your experiences have helped us highlight the doodle breeds that make excellent companions for families with kids.

I would also like to express my gratitude to the dog owners in the sub-niche of service and therapy doodle dogs. Your knowledge about the intelligence, trainable nature, and temperament of these breeds has given us a deeper understanding of the qualities that make them ideal for service or therapy work.

To the dog owners in the sub-niche of sporting doodle dogs, your expertise in various dog sports and activities, such as agility, flyball, or dock diving, has allowed us to showcase the doodle breeds that excel in these areas. Your passion for these activities has inspired us to include comprehensive information for active individuals in search of an athletic doodle companion.

A heartfelt thank you goes out to the dog owners in the sub-niche of doodle dogs for seniors. Your insights into the factors like size, energy level, and ease of training have enabled us to provide tailored recommendations for older individuals seeking a doodle breed that suits their lifestyle.

To the dog owners in the sub-niche of doodle dogs for apartment living, your knowledge about breeds that adapt well to smaller spaces has been invaluable. Your experiences have helped us provide guidance for individuals living in apartments or condos, ensuring they can find a doodle breed that fits their living situation.

I would also like to acknowledge the dog owners in the sub-niche of doodle dogs with unique coat colors. Your expertise in rare or unique coat variations, such as merle, phantom, or parti-color, has allowed us to showcase the beauty and diversity of doodle breeds in terms of their coat colors.

Lastly, I want to thank the dog owners in the sub-niche of doodle dogs with specific coat types. Your knowledge about curly, wavy, or straight coat preferences has helped us cater to individuals with specific grooming and aesthetic preferences.

Once again, I extend my deepest gratitude to all the dog owners who have contributed to this book. Your passion and commitment to your doodle dogs have played a crucial role in making this book a comprehensive and invaluable resource for dog owners in various niches.

14 Most Popular Doodle Dogs*

Even although every dog is unique—just like every human—below are a few stereotypical characteristics of each doodle mix, plus fun facts and what you can typically expect.

1. Goldendoodle[1] (Golden Retriever + Poodle)

---

1. http://www.petmd.com/dog/breeds/goldendoodle

The Goldendoodle first gained breeding popularity in the 1990s. After adoration for the Labradoodle grew and grew, the Goldendoodle was the next obvious choice. This designer dog breed mix has been extremely popular because of the desired traits of athleticism, intelligence, and obedience of both the Golden Retriever and the Poodle.

Weight: 50-75 pounds

Height: 22-25 inches

Lifespan: 8-12 years

Coat colors: brown, red, gold, cream, black, white

Coat texture: curly, medium to long

Personality: friendly, smart, gentle, playful

2. Bernedoodle (Bernese Mountain Dog[2] + Poodle)

These giant, adorable fluff balls were first bred in 2003, solely for the purpose of companionship. Although the Bernese Mountain Dog and Poodle are both traditionally bred for outdoor activities, Bernedoodles are just as happy snuggling up on the couch with you as when they are running through the woods. And their intelligence makes them very easily trainable.

Weight: 70-90 pounds

Height: 23-29 inches

Lifespan: 7-12 years

Coat colors: brown, black, white

Coat texture: curly, long

---

2. https://www.petmd.com/dog/breeds/c_dg_bernese_mountain_dog

Personality: playful, friendly, outgoing, gentle

3. Labradoodle[3] (Labrador Retriever + Poodle)

As the original doodle, the Labradoodle is still one of the most popular doodle breeds. Labradoodles are desirable because both the Labrador Retriever and the Poodle are intelligent and athletic. The Poodle has non-shedding fur, and the Labrador has a laid-back, eager-to-please personality.

Weight: 50-75 pounds

Height: 22-25 inches

Lifespan: 7-12 years

Coat colors: brown, red, yellow, cream, black, white

Coat texture: curly, medium to long

Personality: intelligent, friendly, outgoing, playful

4. Cavapoo (Cavalier King Charles Spaniel[4] + Poodle)

The first Cavapoo was born in the 1990s. Cavapoos are known for being great family dogs because they usually inherit the fur and intelligence of the Poodle, plus the loving nature of the Cavalier King Charles Spaniel. And because of the calm personality of the Cavapoo, they are often used as therapy dogs.

Weight: 8-25 lbs.

Height: 9-14 inches

Lifespan: 10-15 years

---

3. https://www.petmd.com/dog/breeds/c_dg_labradoodle_hybrid

4. https://www.petmd.com/dog/breeds/c_dg_cavalier_king_charles_spaniel

Coat colors: black, gray, red, brown, cream, white

Coat texture: curly, medium to long

Personality: outgoing, playful, curious, gentle

5. Aussiedoodle[5] (Australian Shepherd[6] + Poodle)

The Aussiedoodles first came about in the late 1990s and early 2000s. These adorable pups are well liked because of their widely known goofy and loving personalities. Just keep in mind that they are high-energy and require a good amount of exercise and outdoor activity to keep them mentally stimulated.

Weight: 25-70 pounds

Height: 10-15 inches

Lifespan: 10-12 years

Coat colors: black, red, brown, white, cream, gray, tan, merle

Coat texture: wavy, curly, medium

Personality: loyal, smart, energetic, active

6. Sheepadoodle[7] (Old English Sheepdog[8] + Poodle)

Sheepadoodles are thought to have been started back in the 1960s by the U.S. Army as an experiment because of their intelligence, loyalty, bravery, and intuitive nature. These dogs are also very playful and carefree, which is why they later became a popular companion and family dog in the 1990s.

---

5. http://www.petmd.com/dog/breeds/aussiedoodle

6. https://www.petmd.com/dog/breeds/c_dg_australian_shepherd

7. https://www.petmd.com/dog/breeds/sheepadoodle

8. https://www.petmd.com/dog/breeds/c_dg_old_english_sheepdog

Weight: 60-80 pounds

Height: 16-22 inches

Lifespan: 7-12 years

Coat colors: black, white, gray

Coat texture: curly, medium

Personality: active, friendly, playful, smart

7. Rottle (Rottweiler[9] + Poodle)

The Rottle—sometimes referred to as a Rottie Poo, Rottie Poodle, or Rottie Doodle—is very intelligent and eager to please but can have a stubborn streak. They are highly active and athletic, and need lots of outdoor activity such as walking, running, and hiking. But if they get proper training and plenty of exercise, they will also enjoy curling up next to you at the end of the day.

Weight: 50-90 pounds

Height: 10-25 inches

Lifespan: 8-10 years

Coat colors: black, gray, brown, red, cream, blue, white

Coat texture: curly, medium to long

Personality: playful, intelligent, eager to please

8. Foodle (Toy Fox Terrier[10], Wire Fox Terrier[11] or Smooth Haired Fox Terrier[12] + Poodle)

9. https://www.petmd.com/dog/breeds/c_dg_rottweiler

10. https://www.petmd.com/dog/breeds/c_dg_toy_fox_terrier

11. https://www.petmd.com/dog/breeds/c_dg_wire_fox_terrier

The Foodle came about in the 1990s and is a great pet choice for someone who lives in a smaller home or apartment because of the dog's smaller stature. Foodles are typically good with other pets and children if they are properly socialized. They are known for being alert, attentive, and easy to train.

Weight: 9-12 pounds

Height: 10-11 inches

Lifespan: 10-13 years

Coat colors: black, brown, white

Coat texture: wavy, dense, medium

Personality: smart, courageous, cuddly, active

9. Yorkiepoo (Yorkshire Terrier[13] + Poodle)

Like many other doodle breeds, the Yorkiepoo became popular in the 1990s. Pet parents love them for their intelligence, affection, gentleness, and tiny size—which makes them great for apartment living. Just be aware that they tend to bark a lot.

Weight: 5-15 pounds

Height: 7-15 inches

Lifespan: 10-12 years

Coat colors: brown, cream, black, gray, blue

Coat texture: wiry, curly

Personality: intelligent, affectionate, gentle, outgoing

12. https://www.petmd.com/dog/breeds/c_dg_smooth_fox_terrier

13. https://www.petmd.com/dog/breeds/c_dg_yorkshire_terrier

10. Schnoodle (Standard Schnauzer[14], Miniature Schnauzer[15], or Giant Schnauzer[16] + Poodle)

Schnoodles were first bred in the late 1980s and early 1990s. They make great family pets because they love kids, playing, and getting attention. They are smart, active, easily trainable, and very friendly—but they do tend to bark a lot.

Depending on their size, the Schnoodle can be a lap dog, therapy dog, performance dog, or just a good old family dog. These lovable dogs enjoy being the center of attention.

Weight: 5-70 pounds

Height: 10-26 inches

Lifespan: 8-12 years

Coat colors: Brown, red, yellow, cream, black, gray, white

Coat texture: curly, medium

Personality: Smart, active, friendly, gentle

11. Shih-Poo (Shih Tzu[17] + Poodle)

The Shih-Poo became a popular mix in the early 2000s. Shih-Poos are small, adorable pups with an alert expression. They are playful, friendly, and affectionate—but remember that their size makes them fragile. They will typically enjoy some snuggles and the opportunity to sit in your lap. They are also courageous watch dogs and enjoy barking a lot.

---

14. https://www.petmd.com/dog/breeds/c_dg_standard_schnauzer

15. https://www.petmd.com/dog/breeds/c_dg_miniature_schnauzer

16. https://www.petmd.com/dog/breeds/c_d_giant_schnauzer

17. https://www.petmd.com/dog/breeds/c_dg_shih_tzu

Weight: 7-20 pounds

Height: 8-15 inches

Lifespan: 10-12 years

Coat colors: brown, yellow, black, cream, white, gray

Coat texture: curly, short

Personality: affectionate, cuddly, friendly, intelligent

12. Boxerdoodle (Boxer Dog[18] + Poodle)

Boxerdoodles are a more recent doodle mix, and are known for being playful, friendly, and active. They need a lot of exercise and do best when they have a fenced-in yard where they can run and play. If socialized, they can be great playmates for kids, and they usually love being a family dog. They can range from small to large, depending on their parents' sizes.

Weight: 12-70 pounds

Height: 10-25 inches

Lifespan: 10-12 years

Coat colors: black, gray, red, blue, cream, white, yellow, brown

Coat texture: curly, short to medium

Personality: intelligent, active, friendly, playful

13. Irish Doodle (Irish Setter[19] + Poodle)

The Irish Doodle—also known as an Irish Doodle Setter, Irish Poo Setter, Irish Setterdoodle, or Irish Setterpoo—is known for being a great

---

18. https://www.petmd.com/dog/breeds/c_dg_boxer

19. https://www.petmd.com/dog/breeds/c_dg_irish_setter

hunter and retriever. Irish Doodles are intelligent, active, playful, and sensitive. They make great family dogs and are typically good with children and other pets. Just make sure to keep them physically and mentally stimulated, or they can become destructive.

Weight: 40-65 pounds

Height: 22-26 inches

Lifespan: 8-12 years

Coat colors: cream, brown, black, blue, silver, gray, red

Coat texture: wavy, dense, long

Personality: intelligent, energetic, easy to train, friendly

14. Whoodle (Soft Coated Wheaten Terrier[20] + Poodle)

Whoodles are adorable, smart, and friendly. They make great companion pets, love being active, and can sometimes be a little stubborn. But they are also known for being loving, loyal, goofy, and very affectionate. And they are often compared to the look of a teddy bear.

Weight: 20-45 pounds

Height: 14-20 inches

Lifespan: 8-12 years

Coat colors: black, gray, red, cream, white, yellow

Coat texture: curly

Personality: smart, friendly, outgoing, playful

*Thanks to Victoria Lynn Arnold

---

20. https://www.petmd.com/dog/breeds/c_dg_soft_coated_wheaten_terrier